The Gift To Be Simple

My Answer to a Student's Question

Virgil

Published by Falcon Books Publishing Ltd
Cover design by Tanya Robinson
First Printing: 2020

FALCON BOOKS PUBLISHING LTD
71-75 Sheldon Street Covent Garden.
London, WCH 9JQ

www.falconbookspublishing.com
Copyright © 2020 Virgil
All rights reserved.

ISBN 13: 978-0-9957692-7-4

Ordering Information:
Paperback and ebooks are available on the Falcon Books
Publishing website:
www.falconbookspublishing.com

Dedication

I dedicate this book to all students of the Bardon system who practice only Type 1 and Type 2 exercises.

Thank you in advance for all of the work you will do in the future as adepts.

List of the Author's Titles

The Elemental Equilibrium Notes on The Foundation of Magical Adepthood, Falcon Books Publishing, London. (2017).

The Covert Side of Initiation Falcon Books Publishing, London. (2019).

The Spirit of Magic: Rediscovering the Heart of Our Sacred Art. (Second Edition), Falcon Books Publishing, London. (2019).

Equipoise:: Insights Into Foundational Astral Training by The Franz Bardon Community (Contributing author and organiser), Falcon Books Publishing, London. (2019).

Future Titles

A Tiara of Pearls

God Lived in August Ames

Rewriting Fate

The Covert Side to Initiation (Second Edition).

Contents Page

Preface

A little over a year ago, a message was sent to my Facebook page by an ardent student of the Bardon system. In this message, the student introduced himself, gave me an extensive overview of his background, and then explained that he had been stuck on Step 1 for almost a decade. This message, although long-winded and convoluted, ended with a short and simple question – "Why?" In other words, why had he been stuck on Step 1 for so many years despite his commitment to his training? Why had he been stuck on Step 1 for so many years when other Bardonists were able to work through the entirety of IIH in the same amount of time? Why? Why? Why?

Usually when I am sent a message containing a question, I respond with a message containing an answer. I usually don't respond by writing an entire book, yet the book you are holding in your hands was written over the course of the past eight months in response to that simple one-word question – "Why?"

The student who asked me this question wasn't looking to turn back the clock and regain the ten years he had spent on fruitless training. He knew that wasn't possible. By the time he messaged me, he just wanted to know why. This book is my attempt to give him an answer. It's not a time machine, but it is the best I can do. I hope he finds this answer satisfactory.

Chapter 1

Brahmacharya

Although many yogic texts define brahmacharya as celibacy, this is a very limited and incomplete definition. The word literally means "action done for the sake of realizing Brahma (God)." If all of your energy is spent on actions that bring you closer to God, then none of your energy is wasted. This insight shows what brahmacharya really is; it's not wasting your energy. Yes, having too much sex is a waste of energy. However, many other activities are also a waste of energy. Therefore, it's possible to be completely celibate and still not be practicing brahmacharya. When you waste energy, you have less energy to spend on your magical advancement, and therefore you won't advance as quickly.

I used to be a member of several Bardon forums, and I've seen some pretty silly arguments on them. For example, one time, there was a giant argument over whether or not Bill (William Mistele) had really worked through IIH. Some participants in the argument vehemently insisted that Bill had in fact worked through IIH. Other participants insisted that Bill had never truly worked through IIH. Engaging in these kinds of arguments is a waste of energy, and those who participate in them are not practicing brahmacharya. The yamas and niyamas, which are good spiritual advice in general, are not some arbitrary moral code you should follow because an "authority" tells you to do so. There is a clear logic behind every one of them. Common sense is usually enough to tell you that wasting your energy results in having less energy to devote to your magical training. If common sense isn't enough, then your own experiences should be able to tell you that wasting your energy results in having less energy to devote to your magical training. Either way, you can't help but eventually arrive at the conclusion that wasting your energy is a bad idea.

In addition to getting into silly arguments, thinking too much is another waste of energy. I notice that a lot of Bardonists who are on the beginning steps of IIH frequently think about the work of PME. They can't wait to begin evoking spirits, so they keep thinking about evocation and asking questions about the work of PME on Bardon forums. This is a waste of energy. The energy they spend thinking about the work of PME and asking questions about it should instead be spent working through IIH.

Chapter 2

Time Is Your Most Valuable Resource

*"Time's up. You have had your chance to grow, to
develop, to solve your problems, and to learn to
be free. You have had the chance to make a
contribution to your world. Now the resources I
gave you are no longer available."*

-The Voice of Saturn

Time is your most valuable resource. Annie Dillard
once said "How we spend our days is, of course, how
we spend our lives." If you spend your days on social
media instead of practicing the exercises of IIH, then you will
spend your life on social media instead of practicing the
exercises of IIH. If you spend your days training inefficiently,
then you will spend your life training inefficiently.

You only get 1440 minutes in each day. In his book *15
Secrets Successful People Know About Time Management*,
Kevin Kruse recommends writing the number 1440 on a piece
of paper and taping it over your desk or some other spot where
you will see it regularly. In this way, you will regularly be
reminded that you have a limited amount of time each day.
This will discourage you from wasting your precious minutes
on unnecessary activities. Every minute you spend mindlessly
scrolling through social media is a minute you will never get
back, and that you could have spent introspecting instead.
Every minute you spend reading a commentary about an
exercise is a minute you will never get back, and that you
could have spent actually practicing the exercise instead.

3

Chapter 3

Take Nothing for Granted

There is a fatal mistake that many Bardonists make, and that is taking it for granted that they will successfully work through IIH. Someone who, for some reason, takes it for granted that he will always be healthy will not make an effort to exercise and eat healthy foods. He will think to himself "Why should I bother to exercise and eat healthy foods? Even if I don't, I will still remain healthy." Someone who, for some reason, takes it for granted that he will pass an exam will not make an effort to study. He will think to himself "Why should I bother to study? Even if I don't, I will still pass the exam." The first person is obviously going to suffer ill health, and the second is obviously going to fail the exam. Similarly, only bad things will befall a Bardonist who takes it for granted that he will successfully work through IIH. He will think to himself "Why should I bother training in a focused manner? Even if I don't, I will still successfully work through IIH." He will then train in an unfocused manner, perhaps by practicing lots of useless outside exercises or reading lots of books irrelevant to his training.

There is a book – *The Golden Dawn* – compiled by Israel Regardie. It is a collection of manuscripts related to the Hermetic Order of the Golden Dawn. Since the book is thick and has a black cover, it is usually referred to as the "black brick" in the world of Western esotericism. I was once conversing with a Bardonist who told me that he had recently obtained a copy of the black brick and was in the process of reading through it. I guess this Bardonist took it for granted that he would successfully work through IIH. Otherwise, why would he be ok with reading a book that is completely irrelevant to his training?

When I first began my training, I never took it for granted that I would successfully work through IIH. I knew that it was very possible I would die before completing Step 10, so I did everything I could to maximize the probability that I would complete Step 10 before dying.

In order to maximize this probability, I limited my reading to books that were actually relevant to my training.

There are Bardonists who have looked back at the end of their lives baffled at the fact that they never completed their initiation, despite training for many decades. They failed because they allowed themselves to waste much of their time. They thought to themselves "It's ok if I waste my time reading this book on ritual magic. No matter what, I'm still going to successfully work through IIH in the end." By taking it for granted that they would successfully work through IIH, they fooled themselves into being ok with squandering their most valuable resource.

Do you know that you will successfully work through IIH? No, of course you don't. How can you maximize the probability that you will successfully work through IIH? This is the question you should be asking yourself. It all depends on how you spend your time. If you use your time wisely, you will be more likely to successfully work through IIH. If you use your time unwisely, such as by reading irrelevant books, practicing Type 3/4/5 exercises, or going on social media, then you will be less likely to successfully work through IIH. You can never get the probability all the way to 100%, but you can do all that you can do get it as close to that as possible. Practice only Type 1 and Type 2 exercises. Read only books that are relevant to your training.

Chapter 4

The Five Types of Exercises

[Author's Note: IMO, this is one of the most important chapters in this book. It really captures the philosophy behind my approach to Bardon system training, which emphasizes discrimination and wise/efficient use of one's time]

Although we're only on the fourth chapter, we've already come a long way toward answering the simple one-word question that got me writing this book. So far, we've established that wasting one's energy and time does nothing to maximize the probability that one will successfully work through IIH. We've also established that the reason many people waste their time and energy is that they take it for granted that they will successfully work through IIH, and therefore feel no need to spend that time and energy maximizing the probability that they will successfully work through IIH. However, these insights raise questions of their own. What is and isn't a waste of one's time and energy? How, specifically, can one spend one's time and energy maximizing the probability that one will successfully work through IIH? Yes, I've given general answers to these questions already, but to come up with specific answers, it helps to know about the five types of exercises. They are as follows.

- Type 1: Exercises that are necessary for your magical advancement
- Type 2: Exercises that are extremely helpful
- Type 3: Exercises that are mildly helpful
- Type 4: Exercises that are neither helpful nor detrimental to your magical advancement

- Type 5: Exercises that are detrimental to your magical advancement

When it comes to creating a daily practice routine, my advice is to only include Type 1 and Type 2 exercises. In other words, only include exercises that are necessary or extremely helpful for your magical advancement. All other exercises are a waste of time and energy.

You don't need to go out looking for the exercises that are necessary for your magical advancement. They're all in IIH. If an exercise isn't in IIH, then it's not necessary for your magical advancement.

Repetitious prayer is hands-down a Type 2 exercise. Any good shadow work exercise is also a Type 2 exercise. This is the reason I discuss these exercises in the following two chapters.

If you look at the daily practice routines of those who have spent many years stuck on the beginning steps of IIH, you'll see an abundance of Type 3, Type 4, and Type 5 exercises. If you look at the daily practice routines of those who have worked through IIH in a timely manner, you will see that they consist of only Type 1 and Type 2 exercises, which, if it isn't obvious, is why I recommend only including those two types of exercises.

There are very few Bardonists who practice the exercises of IIH exclusively. This wouldn't be a bad thing if the other exercises Bardonists practiced were all Type 2 exercises. However, more often than not, the other exercises they are practicing are Type 3, Type 4, and Type 5 exercises. If you can't discriminate between outside exercises that are of Type 2 and outside exercises that aren't, then perhaps it is best to stick exclusively to Type 1 exercises. In other words, to practice only the exercises of IIH and no other exercises.

Chapter 5

Type 2 Exercise Examples – Prayer and Repetitious Prayer

Jesus Christ, one of the greatest magicians to walk this Earth, taught his students about the power of prayer. In the Sermon on the Mount, he tells his students "Ask, and it shall be given you." Later in the Gospel of Matthew, he is recorded saying "And all things, whatsoever ye shall ask in prayer, believing, ye shall receive."[1]

Daskalos was another adept who understood the power of prayer. In *The Magus of Strovolos*, Kyriacos Markides records a lecture by Daskalos in which he tells his students "No prayer has ever remained unanswered and no curse has remained unpunished."[2] In an interview transcribed in his book *The Esoteric Practice*, Daskalos asserts that "What is asked for in prayer should be heartfelt, not serving egoism, and dearly desired, for sincere prayer is always heard."[3]

A Unified Mind and Heart

In his essay "The Kabbalistic Secrets of Power Prayer," the Rabbi Ariel bar Tzadok points out that while the Jewish people existed at the time of the Babalonians and Romans, the Jewish people continue to exist today while the Babalonians and Romans are no longer around. In this essay, he reveals a teaching concerning the three tools the Jewish people had at

---

1 Matt. 21:22 (KJV)

2 Kyriacos C. Markides, *The Magus of Strovolos: the Extraordinary World of a Spiritual Healer* (Arkana, 1998), 41

3 Stylianos Atteshlis, *The Esoteric Practice: Christian Meditations and Exercises* (Imprinta, 1994), 7

their disposal to ensure their survival through the centuries. One of these tools is the secret to effective prayer. Sometimes, people repeat prayers that aren't answered. This isn't because prayer is ineffective, but because they are not praying correctly. Correct prayer is effective prayer, and the secret to correct/effective prayer is hidden in the way we clasp our hands together while praying. The right hand symbolizes the mind. The left hand symbolizes the heart. For prayer to be effective, it must be done with a unified mind and heart.

Praying with a unified mind and heart was one of the techniques the Jewish people used in times of trouble, and it served them well because prayers spoken in this manner generate powerful results. Throughout his essay, Rabbi Tzadok discusses several specific examples of this happening. When Jacob was attacked by Esau, he used the power of correct prayer to protect himself. When Haman, the viceroy of King Ahasuerus, plotted to have the Jewish people killed, Esther and her people used the power of correct prayer to protect themselves. When Hannah found herself infertile, she was able to use the power of correct prayer to draw down the divine grace needed in order to become fertile. The Jewish people have the Kabbalah, one of the most potent systems for communing with Divinity and accessing divine power, so it should not be surprising that they understand what it takes for prayer to be effective. However, as Ariel bar Tzadok writes, "The power of prayer is not exclusive to the Kabbalist. Anyone who achieves the proper level of consciousness can achieve the same results from prayer."

Without a doubt, the idea of praying with a unified mind and heart has many layers of meaning, some of which can be profound indeed. As a starting point when it comes to learning to pray with a unified mind and heart, let your heart be filled either with love for God or longing for God, and let your mind be focused firmly on God and know that God is present with you and hears you.

10

Repetitious Prayer

Prayer is a powerful spiritual exercise/technique with many benefits. As I was studying the diverse array of spiritual and religious traditions in the world, I noticed that many of them prescribed a practice consisting of repeating a short prayer over and over again. I have come to call this practice "repetitious prayer." Often, prayer beads are used to count the prayers. For example, the repetition of the prayer "Om Namah Shivaya" is common in many branches of Hinduism, and repetitions are often counted using a rudraksha. Catholics pray the Rosary, which involves repeating the Hail Mary over and over again while using the beads of the rosary to count repetitions. According to Mouni Sadhu, St. Seraphim of Sarov would instruct his students to repeat the Trisagion several thousand times a day. Sufis have a spiritual practice called "dhikr" that has several forms, some of which involve repeating a short prayer over and over again. The reason the practice of repetitious prayer is so widespread is that it has very powerful effects on one's spiritual evolution. I know this from experience.

Doing Repetitious Prayer

I don't think I would have successfully worked through IIH if it weren't for the positive benefits I received from the practice of repetitious prayer. It is my hope that after learning from this chapter how to do repetitious prayer, you will go on to do it yourself so you too can experience those positive benefits.

When it comes to repetitious prayer, the first step is to choose a prayer to use. Ideally, the prayer should be short, so you can easily repeat it over and over again. When I first began engaging in repetitious prayer, I wrote a short prayer that worked very well.

Lord God Almighty, Creator and Maker of Heaven and Earth, please give me wisdom and understanding, please help me become more compassionate, and please help me become a magician. Amen.

Another prayer you can use is as follows.

Almighty Creator, please enlighten my mind and purify my heart. Amen.

Once you have decided upon a prayer to use, you simply have to repeat it over and over again. In IIH, Bardon asks you to create a string of forty beads and to use this string of beads to count the number of times you repeat an affirmation while practicing autosuggestion, the number of breaths you take when practicing conscious breathing or pore breathing, and the number of times you are distracted while meditating. This string of forty beads, which I call a "Bardonian mala," can also be used in your practice of repetitious prayer. Begin by repeating your prayer forty times each day, using the Bardonian mala to count. Consider this one set. Do this for about a week and then increase the number of sets to two per day. After another week, do three sets per day. The sets can be done consecutively but do not have to be.

Chapter 6

Type 2 Exercise Examples - Shadow Work Exercises

In Jungian psychology, the term "shadow" refers to all the aspects of oneself that one has repressed and that one refuses to acknowledge the existence of. For example, if you are repressing a desire for attention, then that desire is part of your shadow. If you are irascible but refuse to acknowledge that you are irascible, then your irascibility is part of your shadow. Carl Jung explained the concept of the shadow quite concisely by stating it is the part of you that you are unconscious of. The process of becoming acquainted with your shadow, transforming it, and integrating its energy back into your conscious self is known as "shadow work." Shadow work is definitely a subject aspiring magicians should look into. In his book *Catching the Thread*, Llewellyn Vaughan-Lee writes the following.

> *We long to stay in the light and keep our darkness hidden, to look towards the heavens and deny the tortuous corridors of our inner self. But all inner work begins with work upon the shadow. It is the basic foundation of any psychological or spiritual path.*[4]

---

4 Llewellyn Vaughan-Lee, *Catching the Thread: Sufism, Dreamwork & Jungian Psychology* (Golden Sufi Center, 1998), 51-52.

In Western esotericism, there is a concept called the "Dweller on the Threshold" which is a thing or entity that prevents people from accessing the deeper mysteries until they are ready to. Bardon states that akasha is the Dweller on the Threshold. Other authors have stated that the shadow is the Dweller on the Threshold. Bardon and the other authors are all correct. The phrase "Dweller on the Threshold" has its origins in literature, not magic/esotericism, and was coined by the novelist Edward Bulwer-Lytton. It was only later that esotericists took the phrase and made it part of the technical language of their field. There are really many things that can prevent immature people from accessing the deeper mysteries of magic before they are ready to, and if we are going to use the term "Dweller on the Threshold" to refer to them, then we must remember that the "Dweller on the Threshold" can refer to any one of these things or to all of them collectively. Akasha can prevent immature people from accessing the deeper mysteries of magic. This is common knowledge, at least among Bardonists, and this phenomenon is frequently discussed in Bardonian literature. The shadow can also prevent immature people from accessing the deeper mysteries of magic. The ultimate source of magical power can be found in the divine spark within us. This divine spark exists at the deepest layer of oneself, so to access its power, one has to journey within. However, when you journey within, you will inevitably encounter your shadow because it is also within you. Unless you have the wisdom, compassion, and maturity to deal with your shadow, you will never get past it and reach the deepest layer of yourself where your divine spark and its power dwell.

In his essay "The Shadow in Psychology and Magick," Bill Mistele explains that becoming acquainted with your shadow is a necessary part of the process of establishing an elemental equilibrium. This makes sense. Establishing an elemental equilibrium involves rooting out your negative traits.

At least a couple of your negative traits are bound to be in your shadow, so the process of becoming aware of those traits is also a process of acquainting yourself with your shadow. That essay is actually one of my favorite essays written by Bill. I highly encourage you to read it.[5]

The bottom line is that a crucial part of spiritual evolution, and therefore of magical advancement, involves confronting your shadow. Bardon never explicitly uses the terms "shadow" or "shadow work" in IIH, but as Bill points out, shadow work is part of the Step 2 astral work and is therefore not missing from Bardon's system. The problem is that when it comes to working with your traits, people only want to deal with the traits they are conscious of. They don't want to deal with the traits they are unconscious of. This isn't surprising; after all, if they were willing to deal with those traits, they never would have banished/repressed those traits into the realm of the unconscious to begin with. In other words, those traits would never have become part of their shadow in the first place. People will move on to Step 3 thinking they have rooted out all of their negative traits but still harboring the major negative traits that are part of their shadow and that they are not conscious of. This is obviously going to cause problems. The astral work of Step 2 requires that you root out all of your major negative traits, including the ones in your shadow.

For this reason, I think it's a good idea for Bardonists who have just begun their training to begin engaging in shadow work. There are many books that contain shadow work exercises. It's worth learning a few that resonate well with you and practicing them. *Romancing the Shadow: Illuminating the Dark side of the Soul*, by Connie Zweig and Steve Wolf, is a good place to start your search. Not everyone who has successfully moved on to Step 3 has studied Jungian psychology or heard the terms "shadow" or "shadow work."

5 http://williammistele.com/shadow.html

However, in some way or another, they have all managed to learn about the major negative traits they are repressing and root those out in addition to the major negative traits they have always been consciously aware of. Shadow work exercises aren't necessary, but I have found them to be very helpful. I consider them to be Type 2 exercises, and therefore worth practicing.

Chapter 7

Mindfulness

Having delved briefly into the subject of Type 2 exercises, I now want to turn to the Type 1 exercises. Specifically, to the Type 1 exercise that is mindfulness. All of the Type 1 exercises are found in IIH. Mindfulness is found specifically in the mental section of Step 1, and is the second of the four exercises in that section.

I discuss mindfulness frequently in my writings, often emphasizing its great importance. For example, in the bonus chapter at the end of the second edition of *The Spirit of Magic*, I explain why mindfulness is the key to mastering the Step 1 mental exercises. That chapter contains important information, but it's a bit long-winded. I'll try to convey the important insights more concisely in this chapter of this book.

First, realize that the four mental exercises in Step 1 are four sides of the same tetrahedron. Therefore, if you get better at one of these mental exercises, you automatically also get better at the other three exercises. For example, if you get better at the second mental exercise (mindfulness), then you will automatically also get better at the first, third, and fourth mental exercises.

You get better at mindfulness by practicing mindfulness, and mindfulness is something you can practice literally every waking moment. If you practice mindfulness every waking moment, your mastery of mindfulness will improve rapidly and your mastery of the other three mental exercises will also improve rapidly as a result. This is why mindfulness is the key to mastering the Step 1 mental exercises. If you've been stuck on Step 1 for many years because you can't master the mental exercises, then there's a good chance you aren't taking the mindfulness exercise seriously enough. Maintain your focus on the present moment at all times, and not just for a few minutes each day.

Bardon devotes only a few paragraphs to mindfulness in IIH. Because the practice of mindfulness is simple, a few paragraphs is all that is needed in order to convey the basic instructions. However, there are also entire spiritual traditions built up around mindfulness and some of these traditions have produced many writings containing useful tips and suggestions for remaining mindful. I recommend looking into them. *Wherever You Go, There You Are*, by Jon Kabat-Zinn, is a good place to start. Earlier in this book, I mentioned a Bardonist who bought a copy of the black brick. The money he spent on that book would have been better spent on Kabat-Zinn's book, or any other good book on mindfulness.

Most people make a half-hearted effort at best when it comes to practicing mindfulness, and then wonder why they've been stuck on Step 1 for years. Instead of trying to remain mindful every waking moment, they spend maybe a few minutes at most each day trying to remain mindful, or maybe even a few minutes every few days. These same people then look in ritual magic books for rituals to practice, or in New Age books for chakra exercises to practice, or in Qabbalah books for pathworkings to practice, all without realizing that what they need is not to practice more outside exercises, but to do a better job practicing the mindfulness exercise that is already part of the Bardon system. Trying to practice all of the Type 3/4/5 exercises in the world won't make up for doing a poor job practicing the Type 1 exercises, of which mindfulness is one.

Chapter 8

The Fifth Precept

L et's say our friend who bought the black brick decides to return it and get his money back. Instead of reading the black brick, he buys some books on mindfulness, or maybe even the Pali Canon itself, and begins to read those. In time, he will learn that according to the Buddha, in order to master mindfulness, it is necessary to hold to the five precepts and overcome the five hindrances. Having learned this piece of useful information, our friend can be satisfied that he did not waste his money buying those books like he would have if he had kept the black brick. If my memory serves me right, the knowledge lectures list the sephiroth of the Tree of Life and the letters of the Hebrew alphabet, but not the five precepts or the five hindrances. The task of a beginning Bardonist is not to learn Qabalah, but to gain rudimentary mastery over his mind.

Having learned of the importance of holding to the five precepts and overcoming the five hindrances, our friend can begin to research methods for doing that. Pema Chodron's book *Living Beautifully* is a decent place to start researching the five precepts. Ajahn Brahm's book *Mindfulness, Bliss, and Beyond* contains useful information for overcoming the five hindrances. It is probably too much of a digression to present a detailed overview of each of the five precepts and each of the five hindrances here, so I will save that for a future book or blog post. However, there is one precept I do want to discuss in depth. That is the fifth precept, which ties in nicely with this book's overall theme of keeping things simple.

The fifth precept is to avoid consuming "intoxicating substances." Traditionally, "intoxicating substances" referred to alcoholic beverages. It's very easy to see why holding to this precept helps one to master mindfulness. You can't be mindful if you're drunk, so the more often you're drunk, the less often you can practice mindfulness. Obvious, right?

In modern times, "intoxicating substances" can be interpreted in a wider sense, and many contemporary Buddhist teachers have commented on all of the other things besides alcohol that can be "intoxicating" in some sense. For example, in an article about the fifth precept, Thich Nhat Han discusses how a lot of the media we are exposed to, including films, television shows, and the news, can be intoxicating. During this discussion, he writes the following.

There may be a lot of violence, hatred, and fear in a film. If we spend one hour looking at that film, we will water the seeds of violence, hatred, and fear in us.[6]

These days, I don't watch a lot of violent movies. However, during my younger years when I did, I distinctly remember feeling mentally and emotionally disturbed after watching them. It was like I had been poisoned in some sense. This feeling of being disturbed would make it more difficult to maintain the inner stillness needed to be mindful or practice meditation.

There is also a lot of crap on social media, and that crap can also be considered "intoxicating." When you consume this crap by spending a lot of time on social media, you are failing to follow the fifth precept. This will impede your efforts to master mindfulness, as well as the other three mental exercises of Step 1. The fourth mental exercise in Step 1 is to still your mind. Spend an entire week without going on social media or watching Netflix or watching television. You will find that it is much easier to still your mind, since you haven't filled it with

---

6Thich Nhat Han, "The Fifth Precept: Diet for a Mindful Society," Bhikshuni Thubten Chodron, accessed June 6, 2020, thubtenchodron.org/2017/11/non-harmful-consumption-not-intoxicants/.

chaotic crap for a long time. Once you go back to consuming the crap on social media and the other forms of media you expose yourself to, you will find that it is much more difficult to still your mind.

I often tell Bardonists not to spend so much time on social media because it is usually a waste of time. However, going on social media isn't just a waste of time. It can be downright detrimental to your progress. You don't have to blindly believe what I'm saying. Take a week-long break from intoxicating media and see for yourself the beneficial effects the break has on your mental training.

The process of letting go of social media, violent films, and other forms of intoxicating media is a process of simplifying one's life, and it will have a decidedly positive impact on your magical advancement. The fifth precept is not just for Buddhists, but for all who seek mental mastery.

Chapter 9

Discrimination

Some people like to come up with cute equations that summarize the factors determining how quickly you advance along the magical path. Here's my equation.

Rate of Magical Advancement = Capacity to Discriminate

This might seem simplistic, but I don't think it is. Yes, it's simple, but not simplistic. It reveals in an extremely clear fashion why some students advance quickly, some advance slowly, and some never advance at all. In fact, if you're someone who's been stuck on Step 1 for years, perhaps you should take some time to really think about this equation. To put the equation into words, it's saying that the better you are at discriminating, the faster you will advance.

You're probably thinking "Wait, you're constantly saying wisdom and compassion are important. How come those aren't in the equation?" Yes, wisdom and compassion are indeed important. However, consider this. If people are wise and compassionate, it's because they did two things.

1.   They discriminated between good uses of their time and bad uses of their time. In the process, they realized that developing important traits was a good use of their time.
2.   They discriminated between important traits to develop and unimportant traits to develop. In the process, they realized that wisdom and compassion were important traits to develop.

In other words, discrimination led to them becoming wise and compassionate. Therefore, it would be redundant to include wisdom and compassion in the equation in addition to discrimination.

What about practicing the exercises of IIH? Isn't that important to do in order to advance along the magical path?

Yes, it is. However, the people who practice the exercises of IIH first discriminated between good and bad uses of their time. In the process, they realized that practicing the exercises of IIH was a good use of their time. It was discrimination that led to them practicing the exercises of IIH, so once again it would be redundant to include practicing the exercises of IIH in addition to discrimination in the equation.

To advance in magic, you need to develop the right traits and practice the right exercises. Discrimination allows you to see which traits are the right ones to develop and which ones aren't. Discrimination also allows you to see which exercises are the right ones to practice and which ones aren't. In the end, the things that get you to adepthood all ultimately arise from discrimination. This is why I equate one's capacity to discriminate with the rate of one's advancement along the magical path.

Here's a list of specific ways the student needs to discriminate throughout his training, including the ones already mentioned. Some of the ways are followed by additional comments.

The student must...

Discriminate between good and bad uses of his time

- This is the single most important way that the student needs to learn how to discriminate.
- Remember → 1440
- Practicing the exercises of IIH is almost always a good use of your time.
- Reading a commentary can be a bad use of your time if you already understand the exercises of the step of IIH you are on and don't need further clarification.
- Discriminate between authors worth looking into and authors not worth looking into
- I've found Bill Mistele, Llewellyn Vaughan-Lee, Stylianos Atteshlis, and Pema Chodron to be worth looking into.
- I'm not going to name specific authors I've found not worth looking into, but a handful are famous esotericists with large followings. See Chapter 23. Don't follow a certain esotericist just because it is the popular thing to do.

Discriminate between books worth reading and books not worth reading

- See Chapter 17 for a bit of guidance)

Discriminate between outside exercises worth practicing and outside exercises not worth practicing[7]

- In other words, discriminate between outside exercise that are of Type 2 and outside exercises that aren't.
- Repetitious prayer and good shadow work exercises are outside exercises worth practicing. They are Type 2 exercises.
- The LBRP is not an outside exercise worth practicing.

Discriminate between effective self-transformation techniques and ineffective ones

- This is obviously important if you're doing the astral work of Step 2, but remember that your efforts to improve yourself don't stop after moving on from Step 2.

Discriminate between small, medium, and large negative/positive traits

- This is obviously true when making your soul mirrors in Step 1, but remember that the student should periodically update his soul mirrors, even after moving on from Step 1.

Discriminate between the useful parts of a book and the less-useful parts of a book

---

7 An outside exercise is an exercise that is not found in IIH, PME, or KTQ. Thus, it is "outside" of the Bardon system. You can practice outside exercises, meaning you don't have to restrict yourself solely to the exercises of IIH, PME, and KTQ. However, if you choose to practice outside exercises, make sure to practice those that are actually helpful rather than a waste of time. This is only possible if you can discriminate between outside exercises worth practicing and outside exercises not worth practicing.

- Mouni Sadhu's book *Concentration: A Guide to Mental Mastery* is divided into three parts. The first two parts are very useful to Bardonists. The third part is not.

Discriminate between the useful sections of an essay by Bill Mistele and the less-useful sections

- Bill's essays are often divided into sections. Some of those sections may be more useful than others. Spend most of your time studying the useful sections.
- The third section of Bill's essay on the Earthzone spirit Cermiel (Preliminary Thoughts) is about how death is perceived and worked with in various spiritual traditions. This section is interesting, but probably won't be super useful to most beginning Bardonists. The tenth section (Cermiel's Outer Aura) is bound to be super useful. There are many important insights in this section that will lead you to wisdom if you reflect on them.

Discriminate between good and bad advice

- If you interact with other Bardonists, then chances are you'll occasionally find yourself receiving advice from them. Sometimes, you'll have a problem and deliberately seek out advice. Other times, Bardonists will offer you unsolicited advice because they think it may be useful to you. In any case, do realize that not all advice you receive will be good. Following bad advice can have negative and even catastrophic consequences.
- In addition to other Bardonists, books can be another source of advice, as can articles and videos relating to

27

the Bardon system. Again, not all advice you receive from these sources will be good advice. Learn to discriminate between good and bad advice.

Chapter 10

Economics vs. Qabalah

Many Bardonists study Qabalah because they think an understanding of Qabalah is something all magicians should have. This is patently untrue. It's a good idea to study Qabalah if it is a major part of the magical training system you are working through, or if you are genuinely interested in the subject. However, don't study Qabalah just because you think magicians should understand it. Again, that's just not true.

If you're looking for a subject to study that is actually useful for Bardonists, my recommendation is to study economics. Consider the following questions.

— What is the opportunity cost of spending five minutes scrolling through a Bardon group on Facebook?
— What is the opportunity cost of spending ten minutes reading a commentary on IIH?
— What is the opportunity cost of reading my book *The Spirit of Magic: Rediscovering the Heart of Our Sacred Art*?
— What is the opportunity cost of reading *The Mystical Qabalah*, by Dion Fortune?
— What is the opportunity cost of reading a chapter of Crowley's *Magick in Theory and Practice*?
— What is the opportunity cost of doing the LBRP?
— What is the opportunity cost of speculating about the spirits of PME for ten minutes?
— What is the opportunity cost of asking a waste-of-time question?

These are important questions for Bardonists to think about, but if you don't have a basic understanding of economics, you don't know what an opportunity cost is and therefore can't even understand these questions, let alone answer them.

For me, the opportunity cost of spending time on social media, including time spent scrolling through Bardon groups on Facebook, is way too high. I'd much rather spend that time practicing the exercises of IIH, conversing with a loved one while I still can because they're still alive (no one lives forever), or working on the novel I'm writing. Writing a novel and getting it published has always been a dream of mine. Allowing social media to drain my time away was never a dream of mine. If you waste all your time and energy on things besides pursuing your dreams, you won't have any time or energy left to pursue your dreams, and you will die unfulfilled. I think many aspiring magicians dream of becoming adepts one day. That dream is within reach. Just use your time wisely.

Chapter 11

Waste-of-Time Questions

Do you know the story of what happened right before the Buddha died? Some guy named Subhadda came to see the Buddha to ask him a question. Buddha immediately realized that Subhadda's question was a waste-of-time question and refused to answer it. Waste-of-time questions are a waste of time to ask and a waste of time to answer. Since the Buddha knew he was dying and didn't have much time left, he chose not to waste his time answering Subhadda's waste-of-time question. Instead, he told Subhadda about the noble eightfold path. This is because he knew that information about the noble eightfold path would be more useful to Subhadda than an answer to his question.

People sometimes asked Ramana Maharshi waste-of-time questions as well. In those instances, Sri Ramana would simply remain silent, refusing to say anything. People also asked Nisargadatta Maharaj waste-of-time questions. In those instances, Sri Nisargadatta would pound the floor with his fist and shout "Kalpana! Kalpana!"

The point is, waste-of-time questions exist. The Buddha, Ramana Maharshi, and Nisargadatta Maharaj refused to answer them because if you answer someone's waste-of-time question, not only are you wasting your own time, you are also encouraging the questioner to continue wasting his time. It is likely he will waste more time thinking about your answer to his question and then come back with follow-up waste-of-time questions.

Sometimes, I get emails or messages containing questions from beginning students of the Bardon system. If the

31

questions are asking for clarity regarding how to practice thought-observation, how to introspect, or things of that nature, then I am happy to answer. However, if the questions are waste-of-time questions, then I don't answer. If you have yet to reach Step 8 of IIH and your question is about the work of PME or KTQ, your question is definitely a waste-of-time question. If your question is about Bardonian avyakata, it is also definitely a waste-of-time question.

Chapter 12
Bardonian Avyakata

The Buddha would refuse to speak about certain subjects because he thought discussion of those subjects was a waste of time, and that instead of thinking about those subjects or discussing them, his students should instead be meditating to obtain the insight that leads to enlightenment and liberation. Those subjects which the Buddha refused to discuss for this reason are called "avyakata" in Buddhism.

There are also topics I refuse to discuss for similar reasons. I call those subjects "Bardonian avyakata." These subjects are somehow related to Bardon or his system; however, time spent thinking about them or discussing them would be better spent actually practicing the exercises of IIH. Here are some subjects that fall into the category of Bardonian avyakata.

- Who Bardon's teachers were
- Whether or not Bardon was the reincarnation of Lao Tzu, Apollonius of Tyana, etc.
- Whether or not Bill Mistele has actually worked through IIH
- How the planes Bardon mentions relate to the four worlds of Qabalah
- How the four elements Bardon mentions (fire, water, earth, and air) relate to the five elements used in Chinese occultism (fire, water, earth, wood, and metal)
- How the steps of IIH correspond to the sephiroth of the Qabalistic Tree of Life

It is clear that these subjects are related to the Bardon system in some way. However, it is also clear that knowing about these subjects isn't going to help you work through IIH any faster. Therefore, I would caution against spending even a single one of your 1440 minutes thinking about or discussing these subjects. There are far better ways to use that precious time of yours.

Chapter 13

Keep Things Simple

H ere in the West, we like complicated things and even value them because of their complicatedness. It's a prominent part of our culture. Not only do we prefer complicated gadgets with lots of apps and features to simpler versions that function just as effectively, we even use the word "sophisticated" as a compliment. Without a doubt, Western esotericism has been heavily influenced by the complicatedness-loving culture it developed in. It's filled with complicated magical theory, complicated rituals, and complicated tools. Since many Bardonists first studied Western esotericism before coming across the Bardon system and recognizing it as their path, they are influenced by the complicatedness-loving attitude that was instilled into them during their prior studies. This often leads them to make things more complicated than they need to be.

One time, I was corresponding with a Bardonist who sent me a picture of the chair he practiced his magical exercises in. There were a bunch of magical symbols drawn on the chair, which confused me. The chair I use for my practices is just a plain wooden chair with no markings on it, let alone magical symbols. When I asked the Bardonist why he had drawn a bunch of magical symbols on his chair, he wasn't able to come up with a good reason for having done so. In fact, he wasn't even able to come up with a reason that sounded good for having done so.

I'm an engineer. Engineers solve problems. In general, engineers prefer implementing simple solutions to problems over complicated solutions. With a complicated solution, there's a lot that can go wrong. With a simple solution, there's less that can go wrong. I've seen many instances in which clients request a complicated solution over a simple solution just because they think complicated is better. Then, the complicated solution goes wrong in a way that creates a big mess and costs the client lots of time and money to clean up. The simple solution would have produced better results, and would have been far less likely to go wrong. It also would've been cheaper.

If your problem is that you need something to sit on when practicing your magical exercises, the simplest solution is a simple plain chair. A more complicated solution would be a chair with a bunch of magical symbols drawn on it. Why use such a chair when a simple chair works just as well. Some magical symbols embody magical energies. What if the energies embodied by the symbols don't harmonize well with each other? In that case, you'd be doing all of your magical exercises while sitting on top of a chaotic energetic mess. That's going to cause problems, and those problems could have been avoided if you'd just left the chair plain and simple. Magic can always go wrong. Energies can always have unexpected side effects, doing things you didn't intend for them to do. It's a bad idea to be drawing magical symbols on random things like your chair unless you have a good reason to. A plain chair might seem simple when compared to a chair with all sorts of sigils and glyphs drawn on it, but it will be better for your practice. Simplicity is something to be appreciated; not something to be destroyed because of a deep-rooted desire for the flashy and complicated.

Chapter 14

Corrupting Bardon's Path

In his book *Alchemy of Light*, Sufi teacher Llewellyn Vaughan-Lee asserts that humanity tends to corrupt things that were originally created for its evolution and development. He gives two examples of this phenomenon. The first example is the early Christian community and the love it embodied and promoted, which eventually became corrupted into a church concerned only with maintaining its power through fear-based manipulation. The second example is the scientific age, which went from reflecting clarity and knowledge to materialism and an arrogant desire to conquer nature.

I see this phenomenon happening with the initiatory path Bardon gave the world through his writings. The path laid out by Bardon is simple and efficient. Yet, since humanity tends to corrupt things created for its evolution and development, it is also corrupting the path Bardon laid out by making it unnecessarily complicated. Don't get me wrong. It's important to personalize the path to fit your individual needs and the unique aspects of your being, but there is a difference between personalizing the path intelligently and corrupting it. I see too many Bardonists doing the latter, and the ways they corrupt this simple and efficient path into a complicated and inefficient one are varied and many.

One good example pertains to the mental training of Step 2, in which Bardon has the student visualizing simple everyday objects like chess pieces, paperclips, or pen caps. When some Bardonists get to this step, they try to visualize Tarot cards, mandalas, or Kabbalistic symbols. Two other examples have been discussed previously. One of those examples is Bardonists drawing magical symbols on their chairs, the cover of the notebook containing their soul mirrors, and other random things for no good reason. The other example is Bardonists adding numerous unnecessary outside exercises to their daily practice routine. If you have an hour every day to practice, why spend the entire hour practicing the exercises of IIH when you can instead spend only five minutes practicing the exercises of IIH and fifty-five minutes practicing banishing rituals, Qabalistic pathworkings, Dzogchen soul-retrieval exercises, yogic pranayama exercises, and Huna energy-work exercises? This seems to be the question many Bardonists ask themselves. It's equivalent to asking "Why walk the path Bardon laid out when I can instead corrupt the path and walk the corrupted path?" Again, I'm not saying you shouldn't personalize the path to suit your individual needs; I did that when I added shadow-work exercises and repetitious prayer into my daily practice routine. What I am saying is that many Bardonists confuse corrupting the path with personalizing it, and that these are not the same thing. Humanity has taken a love-based community and turned it into fear-based one. It has taken a healthy desire for knowledge and turned it into an arrogant desire to conquer. Now it is taking a simple and efficient initiatory path and turning it into a complicated and inefficient one.

These days, much of the destruction humanity has caused in the outer world is seeping into the inner worlds. To rectify the situation, there need to be people who are capable of entering the inner worlds and carrying out work in them. In other words, there need to be initiates. It is imperative that the path of initiation Bardon laid out remain uncorrupted. Each aspiring initiate must personalize the path, but realize that the path Bardon laid out is defined by its simplicity and efficiency.

If you find that the path you are walking has lost any semblance of simplicity or efficiency, then you are no longer walking a personalized version of the path but a corrupted version.

Chapter 15

Just Keep Walking Onward, Even if You Have to Walk Alone

W hen the Bardonists you have acquainted yourself with become interested in Golden Dawn stuff, stay focused on your training. Concentrate on the exercises of IIH. When they say "Practice the LBRP like we do. It's a good supplement to the exercises of IIH," ignore them. Keep pressing forward. Leave them to their LBRP-ing and walk onward toward the completion of Step 10 alone.

When the Bardonists you have acquainted yourself with decide to study Dion Fortune's *The Mystical Qabalah*, stay focused on your training. Concentrate on practicing the exercises of IIH. When they say "You should study this book too because magicians need to know this stuff regardless of what tradition they belong to or which system they are using," ignore them. Keep pressing forward. Leave them to their intellectual studies of Qabalah and walk onward toward the completion of Step 10 alone.

When the Bardonists you have acquainted yourself with decide to practice Reiki, stay focused on your training. Concentrate on the exercises of IIH. When they say "You should also practice Reiki with us because it is a good supplement to the energy work in IIH," ignore them. Keep pressing forward. Leave them to pursue their attunements and walk onward toward the completion of Step 10 alone.

When the Bardonists you have acquainted yourself with become fascinated with Thelema, stay focused on your training. Concentrate on the exercises of IIH. When they say "Bardon quotes Crowley in IIH, so that means Bardonists should practice the Star Ruby each day and dress in black robes," ignore them. Keep pressing forward. Leave them to their Thelemic studies and walk onward toward the completion of Step 10 alone.

When the Bardonists you have acquainted yourself with begin reading the writings of Wilhelm Quintscher, stay focused on your training. Concentrate on the exercises of IIH. When they say "Quintscher was an acquaintance of Bardon, so you should read his writings alongside those of Bardon," ignore them.[8] Keep pressing forward. Leave them to their reading and walk onward toward the completion of Step 10 alone.

When the Bardonists you have acquainted yourself with argue about which commentary on IIH is the best, stay focused on your training. Concentrate on practicing the exercises of IIH. When they say "Come join our argument, because arguing about this particular subject has become a tradition amongst Bardonists," ignore them. Keep pressing forward. Leave them to their arguing and walk onward toward the completion of Step 10 alone.

When the Bardonists you have acquainted yourself with join a new online Bardon forum, stay focused on your training. Concentrate on practicing the exercises of IIH. When they say "You should join this forum too because engaging in online discussions about the exercises of IIH is just as productive as practicing the exercises of IIH," ignore them. Keep pressing forward. Leave them to their discussing and walk onward toward the completion of Step 10 alone.

The fraction of Bardonists who get distracted from their training is large, and therefore, the fraction of Bardonists who complete their training is small. Getting distracted is easier than shooting fish in a barrel. To successfully shoot fish in a barrel, you have to at least make the effort to pull the trigger. To become distracted from your training, you don't even have

---

8See Chapter 17.

to make any effort at all. You just let the distraction take you and carry you away.

Chapter 16

Can Having Little Time to Practice Magical Exercises Be a Blessing?

I t seems like the more time you have to practice magical exercises each day, the better. This is only true for people who know which exercises to practice. If you have a lot of time to practice magical exercises but use that time to practice exercises that are a waste of time, you're not doing yourself any good. People who only have a small amount of time each day to practice magical exercises understand that it is of the utmost importance to identify which exercises are worth practicing and which aren't. Thus, they quickly develop the ability to discriminate between exercises worth practicing and exercises not worth practicing. They practice just the exercises worth practicing because they don't have time to practice the exercises not worth practicing. They experience the benefits of practicing the exercises that are worth practicing, and as a result, they never want to go back to a state of not being able to tell the difference between exercises worth practicing and exercises not worth practicing.

People who have a lot of time to practice magical exercises, on the other hand, might think "I have the time to practice many magical exercises, so I'm going to practice a dozen or more magical exercises each day." They never learn to focus on the two or three exercises most important to them. In the long run, this manner of training will not get them as far as the aspirants who learned to identify the two or three exercises most important to them and focus on those exercises.

Chapter 17

Five Common Mistakes Made When Deciding Which Books to Read

The truth is like a lion. You don't have to defend it. Let it loose. It will defend itself.

-St. Augustine

There are five mistakes many Bardonists make when deciding which books to order on Amazon and read.[9] Those mistakes are as follows.

1. Assuming a book written by a contemporary/colleague of Bardon is going to be useful just because it was written by a contemporary/colleague of Bardon.

2. Assuming a book written by a direct student of Bardon is going to be useful just because it was written by a direct student of Bardon.

3. Assuming a book written by an esotericist who influenced Bardon is going to be useful just because it was written by an esotericist who influenced Bardon.

---

9 Now might be a good time for me to mention that from my point of view, it is my responsibility to share information that is true to the best of my knowledge. It is not my responsibility to push the agenda of any particular esoteric publishing company or esoteric author. Sometimes the information I share may hurt the interests of certain esoteric publishing companies or esoteric authors. While this is unfortunate, I still feel I have a responsibility to share the information anyway.

4. Assuming a book written by an advanced Bardonist (someone who has at least worked through IIH) is going to be useful just because it was written by an advanced Bardonist.

5. Assuming a book written by a well-known Bardonist (e.g. Bill Mistele, Rawn Clark, etc.) is going to be useful just because it was written by a well-known Bardonist.

Books written by contemporaries/colleagues of Bardon, direct students of Bardon, esotericists who influenced Bardon, advanced Bardonists, or well-known Bardonists may be interesting, but being interesting and being useful are two completely different things. My advice is to search for books that are useful rather than books that are interesting. Good books on shadow work (e.g. *Romancing the Shadow: Illuminating the Dark Side of the Soul*, by Connie Zweig and Steve Wolf) and good books on mindfulness (e.g. *Wherever You Go, There You Are*, by Jon Kabat-Zinn) tend to be very useful. One of the best guides to mindfulness I know of is the third chapter of Ajahn Brahm's book *The Art of Disappearing*. However, if you were to ask a typical Bardonist to choose between receiving a copy of Brahm's book for free or paying a lot of money for a book by Wilhelm Quintscher, most would choose to pay for the book by Quintscher.

In Chapter 2, I mention Kevin Kruse's advice to write the number 1440 on a piece of paper and tape it above your desk in order to remind yourself that you only have 1440 minutes in a day. Do you think it would be better to spend those precious minutes reading interesting books or useful books?

Chapter 18

The Books You Need vs. the Books You Want

T he books you want to read are not necessarily the books you need to read. Shortly after I began working through Step 1, I was walking through a Borders in my neighborhood and came across a book about German magical orders. Although the book seemed fascinating, I knew the books I needed to read weren't about magical orders. The books I needed to read were about mindfulness, since this is (IMO) the most important mental exercise in Step 1 and I was absent-minded far more often than I was mindful. After putting the book back on the shelf, I found a copy of Thich Nhat Hanh's *The Miracle of Mindfulness* and bought that instead.

When given the option, I always choose the book I need to read instead of the book I want to read.[10] Of course, I could not do that if I weren't able to discriminate between the books I need to read and the books I merely want to read. This brings us back to the subject of discrimination discussed in Chapter 9.

---

10 When I say I "need" to read a book, what I mean is that the book is extremely helpful. Strictly speaking, the only book anyone every truly needs is IIH.

Chapter 19

Greed

[Author's note: This chapter is an excerpt from a piece I wrote for *Equipoise: Insights into Foundational Astral Training*. I include it here because its subject relates to the theme of this book.]

I have to admit that I used to be a greedy person. Many people think of greed as the desire for more money. In that sense, I wasn't greedy. While I've always had respect for money and its value, I never felt the need to obsess over getting more of it than I really needed. That said, I was still greedy. In Zen Buddhism, greed is seen as the unconditional desire for more, and this is also the way I have come to see greed. Whether a specific instance of greed involves a desire to acquire more money, a desire to read more books, or a desire to have more friends doesn't matter. The belief that more is always better is the root of greed, regardless of whether it is money, books, or friends we are speaking of.

During the summer of 2008, I had the goal of reading two books a week. That's a lot of books to read in one summer. I succeeded because my greed was strong. In other words, I strongly felt that reading more books was better. Later, as I reflected back upon that summer, I realized that I didn't really get anything out of it. What matters isn't the amount of stuff you read (as a greedy person like myself believed), but the quality and thoroughness of your reading. Did you try to consume as many books as possible the way a dragon tries to hoard as much gold as possible, or did you really study each book carefully, taking your time to reflect upon the major lessons within it and extract the key insights?

Consider two Bardonists - Bardonist A and Bardonist B. Bardonist A is greedy. He thinks the more commentaries he has, the better. He spends a lot of effort collecting commentaries. Bardonist B isn't greedy. He doesn't spend a lot of effort collecting commentaries because he doesn't believe that the more commentaries he has, the better. Instead, he is grateful for what he already has, which is just IIH. Because he is grateful for having IIH, he appreciates the book. He seeks to get as much as he can from this one book he has because he understands its true value. Bardonist B is likely to end up with a much more solid understanding of IIH than Bardonist A has, despite the fact that Bardonist A has ten commentaries and Bardonist B has none. More commentaries isn't necessarily better. More of anything isn't necessarily better. Yet, how many people have fully realized this? How many people are truly void of greed?

In the Bardon community, I see a lot of greedy Bardonists. I see people trying to buy more books about the Bardon system because they think more is always better. I see people spending more time practicing the exercises of IIH because they think more is always better. Even as an author, I've had to struggle with greed. When I first started writing, I figured that the more readers I had, the better. Now I realize that it's not about finding more readers. It's about finding the right readers. Similarly, it's not about reading more books about the Bardon system. It's about reading the right books in the right way. It's not about spending more time practicing the exercises of IIH. It's about spending the right amount of time. In other words, enough time to make steady progress but not so much time that you are overtraining and injuring yourself while neglecting other important aspects of your life like your loved ones.

Chapter 20

People Want Your Money

Most people know this already, but if you don't, I'd like to make you aware that there are lots of people out there who really want your money. They'll sell you commentaries on IIH, books about the Bardon system, Bardon-related courses, and things of that sort. Remember, people were successfully working through IIH long before the first commentary on IIH or book about the Bardon system was written. Back in those days, all people had was IIH, and they succeeded in working through IIH because IIH was all that they needed. These days, it's hard to tell if the increasing number of Bardon "resources" in the form of books and commentaries is truly an increasing number of resources or if it's an increasing number of things to be distracted from your training by.

Chapter 21

Why I Don't Discuss the Spirits of PME with People who Message Me

I don't discuss the spirits of PME with people who message me with questions about them. The reason has nothing to do with the fourth power of the sphinx (keeping silence) or anything like that. I just don't want to encourage people to waste their time. People who are at the PME stage of their training can obtain answers to such questions by evoking the spirits of PME or interacting with them through mental wandering. People who are at the IIH stage of their training should be focused on working through IIH. Thinking about the spirits of PME when you are at the IIH stage of your training is a waste of mental energy. It is a failure to practice brahmacharya. Yet, despite all this, I still frequently receive questions about the spirits of PME from individuals who have yet to reach Step 8 of IIH. Here are some examples of just a few of those questions.

> *What methods does Ichdison teach for making wishes come true?*

> *Do the elemental sovereigns mentioned by Bardon (Pyrhum, Istiphul, Parahim, etc.) have a ruler they are all subordinate to, such as the elemental kings mentioned by Eliphas Levi (Paralda, Ghob, etc.)?*

> *What sorts of things does the sylph Parahim like to talk about?*

Each time I am asked a question like one of these, my answer is always the same: "If you are at the stage of your training where it is appropriate to think about this question, then you should be able to obtain the answer via evocation or mental wandering. If you cannot obtain the answer via evocation or mental wandering, then it is too early for you to be thinking about this question."

And yes, as you can imagine, there are always some people who are upset with this answer. I want people to be happy, but I realize that people will be happier if they actually work through IIH than if they fail to work through IIH because they waste all their energy thinking about questions not relevant to their current stage of training. Magic is an art. There is no art that does not demand discipline and focus in order to master it.

Chapter 22

Don't Settle

L et's say you start a romantic relationship with a woman. After a period of dating, you realize that she has a mean personality and you don't enjoy being around her. You end up marrying her anyway because you are afraid you won't find anyone else. You've settled for someone you don't really like, and as a result, you're going to be unhappy for the rest of your life. People do this all the time. They don't really feel happy with their current partner, but they end up settling for their current partner anyway just because they don't believe anyone better will come along. There's no need to condemn yourself to many unhappy years in this manner. Just don't settle.

Let's say you want to learn about the spirit Irumiah, who is one of the ruling genii of the Sphere of Venus. Here are four ways you can gather information about Irumiah.

1. Use evocation or mental wandering to converse with Irumiah.
2. Read a text about Irumiah written by a genuine magician who has used evocation or mental wandering to converse with Irumiah.[11]
3. Speculate about the nature of Irumiah.

---

11 If you have settled for this way, you might find two articles written by Frater Acher to be of interest. The first is titled "A Mirror at an Angel – Or Why Not to Read About Your Holy Guardian Angel." The second is titled "Knowledge is a Sword. Second-hand Knowledge is a Club." Both articles are available online, and it should be easy to find them through a Google search.

4. Read a text about Irumiah written by someone who has never interacted with her, but has merely speculated about her nature.

The first way is the best way. The second way is the second best way. It is better than the third and fourth ways, but inferior to the first way because it can only provide second-hand knowledge.

The third way is a waste of time. The fourth way is also a waste of time, and can lead to arguments. On esoteric forums, you will sometimes see conversations where one person will say "I believe X about Irumiah because it's what John Magus wrote in his book." Another person will reply "Well, I don't believe that. I believe Y about Irumiah because it's what Tommy Mage wrote in his book." Hey, who cares what John Magus or Tommy Mage wrote about Irumiah in their books? What they wrote is all based on speculation anyway. And, on the off-chance that they are an initiate by Bardon's standards and did interact with Irumiah via evocation or mental wandering, the second way of gathering information about Irumiah is still inferior to the first way. No need to argue about which author is right when you don't need either of them because you can interact with Irumiah herself.

Pursue the first way and don't settle for any of the other three ways. The first way is the only way that will provide you with high-quality knowledge about Irumiah. The second-hand knowledge you gain from the second way and the pseudo-knowledge you gain from the third and fourth ways cannot compare with the true knowledge you gain from the first way. Those who go around claiming to know about Irumiah because they've read information about her in the books of John Magus and Tommy Mage are only fooling themselves. They have settled for other ways besides the first way.

Chapter 23

Do What's Wise

The following advice is bad.

Do what's popular.

The following advice is equally bad.

Avoid doing what's popular.

The following advice is good.

Do what's wise, regardless of whether it's popular or unpopular.

There have been fads in the Bardon community in the past, and there will be fads in the Bardon community in the future. It is well-known that Bardon was a practitioner of spagyrics. Let's say that one day, new information about Bardon's spagyrics techniques is discovered, and this sparks widespread interest in spagyrics in the Bardon community. A bunch of Bardonists begin to practice spagyrics because this new discovery has gotten them interested in this subject, and then many more Bardonists begin to practice spagyrics because it's now the cool thing to do and they feel compelled to jump on the bandwagon. Meanwhile, you are a Bardonist on Step 1 of IIH and it seems like all the Bardonists around you are practicing spagyrics. Do you also begin to practice spagyrics, or do you realize that any time you spend practicing spagyrics would be better spent practicing the exercises of Step 1? Hopefully, you choose to do what is wise instead of what is popular. Remember, try to see that your eyes are horizontal and your nose is vertical. When you can see things exactly as they are, you will conclude that spagyrics is best considered a distraction. As a result, you won't be tempted to practice spagyrics, even if all the Bardonists around you are practicing spagyrics. You need to be indifferent to whether an activity is popular or unpopular in order to focus on whether it is wise or unwise. When deciding whether or not to engage in something like practicing spagyrics, doing shadow work, studying Dzogchen, supplementing your training with Huna exercises, practicing repetitious prayer, reading the writings of Wilhelm Quintscher, or whatever, let your decision be based on whether it is wise rather than on whether it is popular.

Chapter 24

No Wonder...

A Bardonist once messaged me complaining that he had been stuck on Step 1 for many years.[12] When I asked him what his daily practice routine looked like, he said it consisted of "thought-observation, psychic healing exercises, a clairvoyance exercise using Tarot cards, the Middle Pillar Ritual, rising on the planes, and the exercises in *A System of Caucasian Yoga*."

In my mind, I thought "Gee, no wonder this guy has been stuck on Step 1 for many years." Without saying outright what the problem with his daily practice routine was, I let him know that I had worked through Step 1 in a timely manner, and that while I was working through Step 1, the only exercises in my daily practice routine were the exercises of Step 1. I hope he understood the point I was trying to convey. Otherwise, he is probably still stuck on Step 1.

Never complain about being stuck on a step for many years. Your advancement is in your own hands. If your advancement were in someone else's hands, I'd consider it reasonable to complain if you find yourself stuck for a long time. However, when being stuck for many years is a result of your own poor choices (like choosing to spend much of your time practicing Type 3, Type 4, and Type 5 exercises), then there is no one to blame but yourself.

---

12 Well, actually, a lot of Bardonists have messaged me about this.

Chapter 25

What's the Mythical Outside Exercise?

I sometimes wonder why so many Bardonists try to stuff numerous outside exercises into their daily practice routine. Perhaps it's because they notice that they have been stuck on Step 1 for many years, realize that they are not making progress through IIH, and think that there is some outside exercise that will allow them to advance quickly through IIH if they practice it. They then shove many outside exercises into their daily practice routine hoping that one of them is this mythical outside exercise.

If you want to know what the exercise that will allow you to advance quickly through IIH is, it's mindfulness. This is the exercise you need to practice if you don't want to remain stuck on Step 1 for many more years.

Now, you might be thinking "Wait, I'm already practicing mindfulness." Are you really though? Practicing mindfulness doesn't mean trying to remain mindful for a few minutes each day, or whenever you happen to feel like being mindful. Practicing mindfulness means remaining mindful every waking moment. Do you try to remain mindful every waking moment? If not, you are dabbling in mindfulness rather than really practicing it.

You can look in Qabalah for a pathworking that will help you move through Step 1 quickly. You can look in yoga for a pranayama exercise that will help you move through Step 1 quickly. You can look in New Age books for a chakra exercise that will help you move through Step 1 quickly. You can look in ritual magic for a ritual that will help you move through Step 1 quickly. However, you'll just be wasting your time. The exercise that will help you move through Step 1 quickly isn't some outside exercise that isn't in IIH and that you need to search elsewhere for. It's the second mental exercises of Step 1. But again, this exercise will only allow you to move through Step 1 quickly if you remain mindful every waking moment.

Chapter 26

Time Spent Mindfully is Not Wasted

Sometimes, you're going to do things that seem like a waste of time. You might spend a few hours looking for a stapler you've lost, only to give up and buy a new one. You might spend a whole day trying to fix a sink, only to give up and call a plumber to do it. You might attend a lecture in which the speaker was clueless and had no idea what he was talking about. You might go to a meeting where nothing productive gets done. These are all examples of instances where you might believe you've wasted your time.

Here's the thing. As long as you were mindful, you didn't completely waste your time. Being mindful improves your ability to focus; after all, mindfulness is simply the practice of focusing on the present. The ability to focus/concentrate is a crucial skill in magic.

I remember one time at work, I had spent a week working on a series of evaluations that I had to fill out by hand. The office where I was working flooded and the papers became illegible. As a result of the flood, a week's worth of work was gone. However, I realized that the time I had spent working on the ruined evaluations wasn't completely wasted. I had been mindful, and so had been improving my ability to focus. The water from the broken pipe that flooded the office may have ruined the papers, but it didn't wash away my improved ability to focus.

Another time, I spent an entire day working to debug some code that it later turns out I didn't need anyway. At first, I thought I had wasted my time. However, I had been mindful the whole time I was debugging the code. As a result, my ability to focus improved, so my time was not wasted.

Time spent mindful is time spent on your magical training. If you've spend the whole day mindful, then you've spent the whole day on your magical training. As you can imagine, this would result in you making rapid progress in your magical training. A day spent mindful is not a wasted day, even if all you did was sit on the couch.

Chapter 27

Throw Out Your Books on Qabalah

I f you've been stuck on Step 1 for many years and have never heard of Jon Kabat-Zinn, you really need to throw out all your books on Qabalah.

Seriously, of the Bardonists I've met who have been stuck on Step 1 for many years, I can't begin to count how many of them know a boatload of facts about Qabalah but have never heard of Jon Kabat-Zinn. The key to working through Step 1 is mindfulness, the second mental exercise. Knowing that Geburah and Chesed are across from each other on the Tree of Life is not going to help you master mindfulness. Knowing that the sephirah Netzach corresponds to the planet Venus is not going to help you master mindfulness either. Jon Kabat-Zinn is a well-known researcher of mindfulness, and his book *Wherever You Go, There You Are* is a decent introduction to the subject. It contains a lot of useful advice that will help you make mindfulness into a way of life and reap the benefits it has to offer.

Again, seek out books that are useful, rather than books that are interesting.

Chapter 28

The Choice Made Every Moment

Every moment, you're confronted with a choice regarding how to use your time. You can choose to use your time wisely, or you can choose to use it unwisely. You can choose to practice exercises that will cause you to progress along the magical path, or you can choose to practice exercises that will cause you to regress along the magical path. You can choose to read books that are relevant to your training, or you can choose to read books that aren't relevant to your training. You can choose to engage in activities mindfully, or you can choose to engage in activities mindlessly. You can choose to make things complicated for yourself, or you can choose to keep things simple.

You are where you are now because of the choices you've made in the past. If you're still stuck on Step 1, it's because of the choices you've made in the past. If you've advanced to Step 8, it's because of the choices you've made in the past. Different people advance through IIH at different rates because they make different choices. To speed up your advancement, make better choices. To slow down your advancement, make worse choices. To keep your rate of advancement the same, continue to make the same choices.

Chapter 29

Self-Respect

Take a moment to think about someone you greatly respect. It could be a parent, a mentor, a great humanitarian, Bardon, or anyone else you look up to. Now tell me, would you ever intentionally waste this person's time?

My guess is you wouldn't. However, if you think about it, it's not uncommon to see Bardonists wasting their own time, perhaps by reading *The Mystical Qabalah* or some other book not relevant to their training, practicing Type 4 and Type 5 exercises, or arguing with other Bardonists about how the steps of IIH correspond with the sephiroth of the Tree of Life.

One possible explanation for this phenomenon is that the Bardonists who engage in such time-wasting activities have a lack of self-respect. You don't waste the time of people you respect, and that includes you yourself. If you truly respected yourself, you wouldn't waste your own time. That goes for everyone.

If you regularly waste your own time, then stop. Learn to have respect for yourself. Do not think to yourself "I am unworthy, and my life is unworthy, so it is ok to squander my life with waste-of-time activities." That is no way for an aspiring magician to think.

Chapter 30

An Erroneous Belief

M any Bardonists erroneously believe that as long as they are doing something Bardon-related, they are advancing along the magical path. As a result, whether they are practicing the exercises of IIH, reading a commentary on IIH, or participating in a discussion on a Bardon forum, they think they are advancing. In reality, the only Bardon-related activity that directly contributes to a student's magical advancement is practicing the exercises of IIH. Reading a commentary on IIH and participating in Bardon forum discussions can contribute to a student's advancement indirectly, but not directly.

Let's say you are on Step 1. When you practice the thought-observation exercise, you advance. If you don't understand the thought-observation exercise and need clarification, you might be able to obtain the clarification you need by consulting a commentary like Rawn's *A Bardon Companion* or by asking about the exercise on a Bardon forum. In this way, the commentary or forum can help you practice thought-observation, thus indirectly contributing to your advancement. However, if you understand the exercises of Step 1 and don't need clarification, then it is better to lock away the commentaries you own and to deactivate your accounts on any Bardon forums.

I once read a poem about how you can tie your shoes in the morning feeling perfectly fine and then be dead before evening. I forget the title of the poem, but it affected me deeply and it often compels me to use my time in the wisest way possible. It is true that you can die at any moment. A car could hit you. A meteor could fall on your head. A mugger could shoot you. You could trip while falling down the stairs and hit your head against the floor. When I die, I want to have advanced along the magical path as far as I could. While I was working through IIH, this thought motivated me to spend more time practicing the exercises and less time reading or on the internet.

Chapter 31

Subconscious Self-Sabotage

I f you've read the second edition of *A Bardon Companion*, then you know that Rawn begins this edition with a discussion of subconscious self-sabotage. Evolution tries to shape all aspects of the human psyche, including the subconscious, into the form that is most conducive to survival. Therefore, the subconscious is programmed to resist change. Change means things are going to be different. Different means unknown. Unknown means possibly dangerous. From an evolutionary point of view, it makes sense that the subconscious is programmed to resist change. It does this by influencing us to avoid change or sabotaging us when we consciously seek change.

The thing is, as Rawn explains, the work of IIH will change you. By practicing the exercises of IIH, you are changing yourself. This can result in your subconscious sabotaging your efforts to work through IIH. Rawn gives a few examples of this sabotage. One example he gives is misplacing your copy of IIH so you can't read the instructions for exercises and practice them. You might think this is ordinary messiness and forgetfulness, but it could also be that your subconscious subtly influenced you into misplacing the book. Another example Rawn gives is going to bed too late so you can't wake up early the next day to practice the exercises of IIH. This might seem like a standard case of poor decision making, but it could also be that your subconscious sabotaged you by subtly influencing you into going to bed late.

One other way the subconscious sabotages you is by getting you to read books about the Bardon system or discuss the Bardon system with others instead of practicing the exercises of the Bardon system. In PME, Bardon discusses various magical tools like the wand, the sword, and the pentacle. Let's say that you are on Step 1 of IIH and someone writes a book that gives a detailed analysis of Bardon's comments on these tools. You might go buy the book and read it. Why? Well, your subconscious successfully influenced you into doing this. Your subconscious knows that if you are reading this new PME-related book, then you aren't practicing the exercises of IIH, and therefore you aren't changing yourself. Every time a new book related to the Bardon system comes out, you can be sure that your subconscious will try to influence you into reading it.

Let's say you feel the urge to log into a Bardon forum and discuss the Bardon system. You turn on your computer, log into the forum, and spend some time reading posts and replying to the posts. Perhaps you even make a new post or two yourself. Before you know it, the sun has set and you are left wondering where the afternoon went. All the time you had previously planned to spend practicing the exercises of IIH is now gone and you can't get it back. Once again, your subconscious has been successful in its efforts to sabotage you.

Of course, your subconscious can also sabotage you by influencing you into practicing Type 3/4/5 exercises or making your training unnecessarily complicated in any of the other ways we've discussed throughout this book so far. Given the large number of ways your subconscious can sabotage your efforts to work through IIH, it might seem like working through IIH is impossible. Actually, that is far from the case. As Rawn explains, if you truly commit from the bottom of your heart to working through IIH, then your subconscious will see that it is futile to sabotage you and will cease to do so. All of the people who are being sabotaged by their subconscious minds into reading unnecessary books about the Bardon system and spending more time online than in meditation simply have not truly committed to the Bardon system yet.

Chapter 32

Vasanas

Some people believe that those who spend a lot of time reading books about the Bardon system or discussing the Bardon system with others online are really dedicated to their training. Actually, the opposite is true. The tendency to spend a lot of time reading books about the Bardon system is a vasana. The tendency to spend a lot of time discussing the Bardon system with others online is also a vasana. If you are really dedicated to your training, your dedication should be strong enough to overpower these vasanas. Only those who spend a lot of time practicing the exercises of the Bardon system are really dedicated to their training.

When you give in to a vasana, you strengthen that vasana. In the third mental exercise of Step 1, we are told to concentrate. In the fourth mental exercise of Step 1, we are told to keep the mind still. Vasanas disturb the mind, preventing it from concentrating or remaining still. Do not give in to your vasanas.

Chapter 33

See That Your Eyes are Horizontal

In Japan, there are three main schools of Zen Buddhism - the Rinzai school, the Soto school, and the Obaku school. The founder of the Soto school, Dogen Zenji, was an interesting person. Throughout his life, he was able to produce many miracles as a result of his high level of spiritual attainment. What I want to discuss in this chapter, however, is not the miracles he produced, but something much more important – a statement he made that many aspiring magicians will find helpful.

In the year 1212, Dogen Zenji became frustrated with the infighting and unfulfilling teachings of the school of Buddhism he had been initiated into. Seeking a more pure form of Buddhism, he traveled to China and studied there for over a decade before returning to Japan. When he finally returned to Japan, he was asked what he had learned. His reply was "I have learned that my eyes are horizontal and my nose is vertical." This may seem like a strange answer, but it contains an incredibly useful teaching. According to Zen teacher Barbara Shoshana, this was Dogen Zenji's way of saying that he had learned to see things exactly as they are.

I think Bardonists should also learn to see things exactly as they are. Imagine if someone was digging around Bardon's old house and found an unpublished manuscript for a book about spagyrics, and that after being found, this manuscript was then published as a book. Quite a few Bardonists would think to themselves "OMG that's a must-have! I absolutely NEED a copy!" Of course, these Bardonists only think that because they can't see the book exactly as it is. What gets in the way when we try to see something exactly as it is?

Assumptions, preconceived notions, conceptual thinking in general... In this case it might be the assumption that every book that was written by Bardon is a must-have. Or, perhaps it is the preconceived notion that if a book was written by Bardon, it is going to be useful. What happens when you get rid of your assumptions and preconceived notions? You don't see a must-have instead of the book. You see the book, and you see it exactly as it is. Only then can you make an informed decision regarding whether or not you should buy it.

Your decisions, including your decisions regarding how to spend your time and money, are based on the information you have. You acquire information through observation. If you can't see things exactly as they are, then the information you are acquiring through observation is distorted and misleading. You need to be able to look at everything related to the Bardon-aspect of your life and see it exactly as it is. What should you do with it? How much money should you spend on it? How much time should you spend using it? When you see things exactly as they are, the answers to these questions become clear.

Chapter 34

Pooping Mindfully Costs Nothing

I magine a hypothetical situation in which an advanced Bardonist writes and publishes a book about the similarities between Quabbalah and Tantra. I'm sure a lot of students on the beginning steps of IIH would buy this book, even though reading the book would not cause them to advance along the magical path.

According to a survey carried out by Verizon, 90% of people take their phones with them into the bathroom. When they poop, these people mindlessly scroll through social media, look at memes on Reddit, or surf the web.

Imagine if you were to refrain from taking your phone with you into the bathroom, and to just poop mindfully instead. It costs nothing to do this. In addition, since mindfulness is a Step 1 mental exercise, every second that you poop mindfully is a second you are advancing along the magical path.

Many of the same students of IIH who would pay money for a book about Quabbalah and Tantra do not poop mindfully, even though reading a book about Quabblah and Tantra will do nothing for their magical advancement and pooping mindfully will bring them further along the magical path.

It's not uncommon for people to spend half an hour pooping each day, especially if they go more than once. Remember, there are only 1440 minutes in a day, and you should not let even one of those 1440 minutes go to waste. This means you shouldn't let the thirty minutes you spend sitting on the toilet go to waste. When you poop mindlessly as you sit absorbed in your phone, you are letting those minutes go to waste. When you poop mindfully, you are using those minutes to advance along the magical path. Again, and I cannot stress this enough, it costs literally nothing to do this.

So the next time you desire to buy a book about magic, ask yourself "Do I poop mindfully, or do I take my phone with me into the bathroom?" If you don't poop mindfully, then try pooping mindfully before you try reading yet another book in your attempt to become a magician. Mindful pooping is free. No need to give Amazon your credit card information.

Chapter 35

Peeing Mindfully Also Costs Nothing

J ust before sitting down to write this chapter, I went to the bathroom to pee. I took my phone with me, not so I could scroll through Facebook while peeing, but so I could time how long it took me. It took me around ten seconds (not counting washing/drying my hands).

When you pee, you should pee mindfully. Whenever you are mindful, you are advancing along the magical path. You might think to yourself "The amount of advancement that comes from remaining mindful for ten seconds is small, so I will not bother. I will just pee absent-mindedly." If this is the case, you have the wrong attitude.

Let's say your goal is to have a million dollars and someone offers you ten pennies. Should you accept the pennies? Of course! Don't think to yourself "This is a trivial amount of money, so I am going to be contemptuous of it and not accept it." If you are offered even one penny, you should accept it because even one penny will take you closer to your goal.

Don't be contemptuous of the small amount of magical advancement you gain for remaining mindful during the ten seconds it takes you to pee. You should be mindful every waking moment, and this includes every moment you are in the bathroom.

Chapter 36

Stop Saying "No" to Magical Advancement

S tephen Covey, a renowned expert in management and productivity, likes to point out in his writings that saying "yes" to one thing means saying "no" to something else. If you don't understand what this means, imagine that you have five minutes of free time. If you spend these five minutes online reading posts, commenting under posts, and making your own posts on a Bardon forum, then you cannot simultaneously use these minutes to practice meditation, visualization, or pore breathing. Of course, doing things on a Bardon forum will not result in magical advancement, but practicing magical exercises will result in magical advancement. When you say "yes" to spending your time on a Bardon forum, you are at the same time saying "no" to magical advancement.

Go onto any Bardon forum and look at the users that are currently online. At this moment, those users are saying "no" to magical advancement. If you wish to work through IIH, then I encourage you to say "yes" to magical advancement as often as possible.

This is a book about simplicity. The fewer activities there are in your life, the simpler your life will be. Therefore, get rid of unnecessary activities. Chit-chatting online about how the ten steps of IIH line up with the ten sephiroth of the Tree of Life is an unnecessary activity. Say "no" to this sort of thing so you can say "yes" to magical advancement instead.

Chapter 37

Cause and Effect

You need to understand, appreciate, and frequently take into account the principle of cause and effect. Causes in the past will produce effects in the present. The following are some examples of this phenomenon.

This morning, I listened to a song on my iPod. Now, it is stuck in my head and making it harder to meditate.

I spent a lot of time watching television yesterday. Today, I have to catch up on work I didn't do yesterday, leaving me with no time to practice the exercises of IIH.

A week ago, I practiced the elemental pore breathing exercises of Step 3 even though I knew I hadn't established an elemental equilibrium. Today, I am much more irascible and jealous than I was last week. Furthermore, my general anxiety disorder has gotten worse.

I went to bed really late last night. I am struggling to stay awake while meditating right now because I am sleep-deprived.

Causes in the present will produce effects in the future. The following are some examples of this phenomenon.

Right now, I am listening to a song on my iPod. It will be stuck in my head when I try to meditate later this evening.

Right now, I am watching television. Tomorrow, I will have to catch up on work I didn't do today because I am watching television, leaving me with no time to practice the exercises of IIH.

Right now, I am practicing the elemental pore breathing exercises of Step 3, even though I know I haven't established an elemental equilibrium. A week from now, I am going to be much more irascible and jealous than I am now. Furthermore, my general anxiety disorder will be worse.

I am staying up late right now. Tomorrow, I will struggle to stay awake while meditating because I will be sleep-deprived.

The best way to gain an appreciation for the principle of cause and effect is to keep a cause and effect journal for a period of time, perhaps a month or so. Buy a notebook. Every time you encounter a problem in your training (e.g. not having enough time to practice, falling asleep while meditating, having a song stuck in your head while meditating, etc.) write down the problem and list the cause(s) that produced the problem. Also, anytime you make a decision you know is unwise, record the decision and list the future negative effects that you expect the unwise decision to produce.

If you adopted an unnecessarily complicated approach to magical training in the past, you are probably experiencing the negative effects in the present. If your current approach is simple but you change it to make it unnecessarily complicated, you will experience the negative effects of this choice in the future. Your past self should have kept things simple in order to avoid causing problems for your current self. If your past self didn't do this, then I encourage you to be more considerate of your future self than your past self was of you. Starting right now, adopt an approach to magical training that isn't unnecessarily complicated to avoid causing problems for your future self.

Chapter 38

Assertiveness

It's important to learn to be assertive. There are at least three good reasons for this.

1. Assertiveness prevents you from hurting others when others cause problems for you.

W hen others cause problems for you, there are four courses of action you can take.

The first course of action is to do nothing, which is not advisable because then they are going to continue causing problems for you. You don't want to be the kind of person that others can just step all over.

The second course of action is to react aggressively. This course of action is also not advisable, and it is not advisable for many reasons. One of the biggest reasons is that you might hurt those who are causing problems for you. This is obviously the case if you are physically aggressive, but also the case if you are verbally aggressive.

The third course of action is to react passive-aggressively. This course of action is not advisable for the same reasons the second course of action is not advisable. Passive-aggression is still a form of aggression.

The fourth course of action is to respond assertively. This course of action is advisable because you will solve the problem without becoming angry and without hurting anyone.

2. Assertiveness will prevent you from wasting your time because it will make you comfortable saying "no" when others ask you to do stuff you're not obligated to do (e.g. favors).

I often use this story to illustrate why it's important to develop assertiveness, so if you correspond with me often, you've probably heard it before. It's not the first time my inability to say "no" caused me to hate myself, but it was the time that finally caused me to snap and do something about my passiveness.

When I was in college, I had a roommate who belonged to a fraternity. His fraternity had printed a bunch of pictures on sheets of paper and wanted him to cut the pictures out. That was a lot of work. As he sat at his desk cutting out the pictures, he asked me if I was busy. I said I wasn't, so he asked me to help him cut out the pictures. Since I already said I wasn't busy, I felt bad about saying no, so I agreed to help him. As a result, I wasted half an hour of my time cutting out pictures for a fraternity I didn't care about to help a guy I didn't particularly like. While it was true I wasn't busy, there was still stuff I could've been doing, and that I would have preferred to be doing than cutting out pictures. Furthermore, even if I had had nothing better to do, I still wouldn't have been obligated to help my roommate, and would still have retained the right to say "no" to his request. Of course, I didn't know this at the time, but learned shortly afterwards when I began to study assertiveness. Those who know me are well-aware that I am the kind of person who doesn't like to waste even a minute of his time, so you can imagine that wasting thirty minutes of my time because I wouldn't say "no" really underscored how big of a problem my lack of assertiveness was.

I wasn't a student of magic back then, but if I had been, then those thirty minutes were minutes I could have used to practice the exercises of IIH. Instead, I wasted them cutting out pictures. I'm not saying you should never do favors for others. If you have a friend who's in trouble and needs help from you, then definitely consider helping him/her. Friends should be able to depend on each other when they are in need. But this doesn't mean you have to say yes every time a friend, acquaintance, or coworker asks you for a favor. You have to be protective of your time or people will take advantage of you and you won't have any time left to practice your magical exercises.

3. **A lack of assertiveness reflects a weakness of the fire element in the personality, and therefore a lack of elemental equilibrium.**

Assertiveness is one of the most important qualities corresponding to the fire element. If you are not assertive, then the fire element in your personality is weak, and therefore you are unbalanced.

Chapter 39

Don't Get Snared

Better to shun the bait than struggle in the snare.

-William Blake

The Devil is constantly trying to ensnare people. No, I don't mean the Christian Devil who is a red humanoid creature with horns on his head and a pitchfork in his hand. In some traditions of Western esotericism, the Devil refers to the impersonal force which tries to keep people in ignorance, and which people must struggle against if they are to attain wisdom and become enlightened. In struggling against the Devil, one also becomes strong, and so power is gained in this way as well as wisdom.

The Devil's snares are designed to keep us from making progress along the magical path. Fun outside exercises that don't really supplement our Bardon system training and interesting books not relevant to us at our current stage of training are two of the most common forms of bait the Devil uses to ensnare us in a habit of wasting our time - time we could be spending practicing useful exercises and reading books relevant to us at our current stage of training.[13]

Shun the bait. To do this, it is imperative to see the bait for what it really is. No matter how fun or interesting bait may be, its ultimate purpose is to get you into a snare, thus trapping you and halting your progress.

13Remember, not every book related to the Bardon system is relevant to you at your current stage of training.

Chapter 40

Don't Become Intellectually Overweight by Reading Too Much

I n his book *The Art of Disappearing*, Ajahn Brahm discusses the problem of reading too much. He points out that modern day Buddhists have access to hundreds of recorded lectures and translations of the suttas. He reminds readers that during the time of the Buddha, a typical Buddhist would have heard maybe one sutta, and that this was enough to help them see the truth. During this discussion of excessive reading, Ajahn Bram remarks "Just as many people's bodies are overweight and obese because they eat too much, so too, many people's brains are overweight and obese because they ingest too much information."[14]

This problem of intellectual obesity is also an issue in the esoteric world. In his book *Spiritual Alchemy*, Robert Ambelain discusses the seven deadly sins. One of the sins is gluttony, which is often thought of as eating too much food. In Ambelain's description of gluttony, he states that this quality causes the aspirant "to devour those documents, books, treatises, and schemes which are accessible to him without control." When I first read that passage, I realized that I was a glutton. When it comes to physical obesity, some people have illnesses or conditions that cause them to continually gain weight. In fact, Bardon himself had such an issue. His thyroid condition caused him to continually gain weight. However, when it comes to being intellectually overweight, you really can't blame such illnesses or conditions. The good thing is that

---

14 Ajahn Brahm, *The Art of Disappearing: The Buddha's Path to Lasting Joy* (Wisdom Publications, 2011), 124

being intellectually overweight doesn't have to be a permanent problem. However, the first step to solving this problem is to admit that you have it. From there, it may be a good idea to find a replacement activity for reading. In other words, find a use for the time you otherwise would spend reading. The practice of Type 1 and Type 2 exercises is a good use of that time.

Chapter 41

Acquiring vs. Letting Go

One of the biggest mistakes Bardonists make is thinking they need to acquire the things necessary to advance along the magical path. They acquire more books, they acquire more outside exercises, they acquire more memberships on Bardon forums, etc.

Usually, what they actually need to do is let go of the things keeping them from advancing along the magical path. Let go of your tendency to spend more time reading than practicing. Let go of your habit of reading the books you want to read instead of the books you need to read. Let go of all the Type 3, Type 4, and Type 5 exercises that are currently part of your daily practice routine. Let go of your accounts on various Bardon forums so you can spend more time in your meditation room and less time online. Let go of your tendency to spend too much time on social media. Or, let go of your resistance to admitting to yourself that you spend too much time on social media.

Zen Buddhism teaches the immense value of letting go. I sometimes get messages from Bardonists telling me they plan to buy my book *The Spirit of Magic* (the most popular and well-known of my books). When this happens, I usually ask them a few questions about their approach to IIH. After reading their responses, I often find that their approach is unnecessarily cluttered. In these instances, I discourage them from buying and reading my book, and I encourage them to use their time to study Zen Buddhist teachings instead. *The Spirit of Magic* was really written for people who are completely new to magic, and it gives a basic overview of magical philosophy. If you've been practicing IIH for more than two years, you probably already know most of the information in it. However, many Bardonists are still stuck in a mindset of acquiring rather than a mindset of letting go, and so they never let go of the things holding them back and preventing them from advancing. Instead of acquiring yet another book related to the Bardon system to add to the hoard of books they've previously acquired, I think it would be better for them to begin learning to let go. *The Spirit of Magic* doesn't teach you how to do that, but some books on Zen Buddhism, such as Barbara Shoshana's *Zen Miracles*, do. We are conditioned to think that acquiring is productive, and that he who has more is worth more and better off. Part of this conditioning comes from modern consumer culture, but it also has deep biological roots. During the days when we were hunter-gatherers, hunting down more animals and gathering more berries made you less likely to starve to death. Times have changed, and even though we have kept this instinctive desire to always acquire more, this desire is no longer as useful as it once was. Really, letting go is often more productive than acquiring. In those instances when you acquire Type 3, Type 4, and Type 5 exercises or books filled with Bardonian avyakata that you plan to read, acquiring is downright counterproductive.

The next time you are about to add an exercise to your daily practice routine, ask yourself "Do I really need this exercise, or am I only adding it because I am conditioned to acquire?" The next time you are about to buy a book about the Bardon system, ask yourself "Do I really need this book, or am I only buying it because I am conditioned to acquire?" Be mindful of your motivations for acquiring. You will find that you often acquire because you are impulsively compelled to, and not because there is a good logical reason to acquire.

Chapter 42

Common Sense

Much of the stuff in this book is common sense. I often tell people to seek out wisdom. That's good advice, but you should also know that a lot of the time, common sense suffices. The reason I felt a need to write a book containing mostly common sense is that common sense, despite its name, really isn't that common. If it were, Bardonists would spend more time practicing the exercises of IIH and less time discussing Bardonian avyakata or practicing Type 3/4/5 exercises. Bardonists would also spend much less money buying books and commentaries they don't really need.

When the Bardonists around you reveal that they lack common sense, don't give up your own common sense in order to fit in with them. Instead, continue to listen to your own common sense all the way to adepthood.

Chapter 43

Travel Light

He who must travel happily must travel light.

-Antoine de Saint-Exupery

To travel happily on the magical path, it is best to travel light. This means not weighing yourself down with unnecessary clutter. Some Bardonists find the Golden Dawn system interesting and try to work through the Golden Dawn system while they are simultaneously trying to work through IIH. Other Bardonists draw magical symbols on the chair they practice in, the notebook they use for their soul mirror work, their string of forty beads, and every other object related to their training. Other Bardonists include a bunch of Type 3, Type 4, and Type 5 exercises in their daily practice routine. Other Bardonists sign up for memberships on various Bardon forums that aren't all that useful. These are all examples of weighing yourself down with unnecessary clutter.

I once conversed with a Bardonist who told me about a wand he recently made. This Bardonist was on Step 2 of IIH. Why does a Bardonist on Step 2 of IIH need a wand? The wand is just more clutter to weigh him down and prevent him from traveling light as he journeys to Step 10 and beyond. Consumer culture is heavily prevalent in the West. It makes us desire a bunch of crap we don't really need, whether it is exercises, books, tools, symbols, or whatever. Get rid of the stuff you don't need, whether it is unnecessary exercises in your daily practice routine, or books that aren't really useful (despite their authors being famous esotericists or even famous Bardonists), or ritual tools you aren't qualified to work with at your current stage of training, or symbols that do nothing but make your chair and journal look flashy. These things just weigh you down and prevent you from travelling light.

Chapter 44

Three Common Mistakes Made When Deciding What Outside Exercises to Practice

There are three mistakes many Bardonists make when deciding what outside exercises to practice. These mistakes are as follows.

1. **Assuming an exercise will be helpful just because it is interesting**

Being interesting and being helpful are two entirely different things. There are many interesting exercises out there, but not all of them are helpful. An exercise can be interesting for many reasons. It can be interesting because it involves visualizing mysterious symbols and chanting mysterious names. It can be interesting because the person who created the exercise was a famous occultist. It can be interesting because it is controversial. It can be interesting because it comes from an exotic spiritual tradition. It can be interesting because the book the instructions are given in is rare and hard to find. Regardless of why an interesting exercise is interesting, being interesting does not mean it is useful.

2. **Assuming an exercise will be helpful just because it is popular**

Don't assume an exercise will be helpful just because it is popular amongst Bardonists or popular in the esoteric world in general. You might be asking "If an exercise isn't helpful, why would it be popular?" The answer is that many, perhaps even most, students of magic are bad at discriminating between the five types of exercises discussed in Chapter 4. Therefore, it's not uncommon to see Type 3, Type 4, or even (especially?) Type 5 exercises being widely practiced.

3. Assuming an exercise will be helpful just because it was created by an advanced Bardonist

Rawn Clark has created a number of exercises, including the Eight Temples visualizations, the Magic of IHVH-ADNI energy exercises, the Center of Stillness meditations, and the elemental regions exercise posted on his website. Bill Mistele has also created a number of exercises, including the sea of love meditation, the sea of fire meditation, and the electromagnetic ball exercise. Just because an exercise was created by an advanced Bardonist doesn't mean it will be helpful. Often, these exercises were designed to fulfil a specific purpose. For example, the sea of water meditation was designed to help practitioners develop the positive qualities corresponding to the water element (e.g. empathy). That purpose may or may not be relevant to you at your current stage of training. In my experience, the sea of fire meditation is actually really dangerous unless you have thoroughly purified yourself of any negative fire traits (e.g. irascibility, hatefulness, jealousy, etc.) I strongly advise against practicing it until you have made significant progress in your magical advancement.

The outside exercises you want to be practicing are Type 2 exercises. Whether or not an outside exercise is a Type 2 exercise has nothing to do with whether or not it is interesting, popular, or created by an advanced Bardonist. Nishkama karma, for example, is not particularly interesting, it's not popular (I've never seen it discussed on a Bardon forum), and it definitely wasn't created by an advanced Bardonist. It is a Type 2 exercise though.

Chapter 45

How to Never Work Through IIH

I f you want to ensure you never work through IIH, you're in luck! All you have to do is follow the instructions below.

1. Start by including only the exercises of IIH in your daily practice routine.

2. Add some exercises from Huna to your daily practice routine.

3. Add some exercises from the various New Age books you've read to your daily practice routine.

4. Add some pseudo-Kabbalistic exercises to your daily practice routine.

5. Add the LBRP to your daily practice routine.

6. Add some Vajrayana visualization exercises to your daily practice routine.

7. Add some qigong exercises to your daily practice routine.

8. Add some scrying exercises to your daily practice routine.

9. Add some planetary invocations to your daily practice routine.

10. At this point, because of all the other stuff you've added to your daily practice routine, you will no longer have time to practice the exercises of IIH. Since you can't work through IIH if you don't practice the exercises of IIH, this means you will never work through IIH. Congratulations! You've just joined the

ranks of the hundreds of other "Bardonists" who were distracted from the path by the myriads of shiny stuff in the occult world and never completed their training.

Chapter 46

Raga

The five kleshas which create pain in the long term and destroy our progress are avidya, asmita, raga, dvesha, and abhinivesha. Raga is attachment.

Sometimes, I'll tell a person to let go of an outside exercise he is practicing. In other words, to drop it from his daily practice routine and no longer practice it. Often, the person will then become upset with me and refuse. It's not because he has some logical reason to continue practicing the exercise; I have already used logic to show why any time spent practicing that exercise would be better spent practicing the exercises of IIH. It's because he has become attached to that exercise. This is an instance of raga. The magical path takes us to fulfillment. When attachments like this prevent us from advancing along the path, they keep us in a state of being unfulfilled. Attachments can destroy our progress. It's no wonder that the word "klesha" (poison) is used to describe raga.

When you let go of unhelpful outside exercises, you can devote more time and energy toward mastering the exercises within IIH.

Chapter 47

Identical Fractions

S tep 1 shouldn't take too long if you are practicing seriously. Practicing seriously means practicing all of the exercises seriously. This includes the second mental exercise of Step 1 – mindfulness. Practicing mindfulness seriously means trying to remain mindful every waking moment. What fraction of Step 1 Bardonists try to stay mindful every waking moment? What fraction of Step 1 Bardonists are moving through Step 1 in a timely manner? Is it some strange coincidence that the two fractions are pretty much identical?

No. It is neither strange nor a coincidence at all.

Chapter 48

The Arts and Crafts Store

Not too long ago, an arts and crafts store located a block from where I live went out of business. Shortly before closing, they had a clearance sale. I went in to check it out and was amazed by how big the discounts were. They were selling all the items in their jewelry-making section at an 80% discount. These items included beautiful glass and ceramic beads. Each glass bead was translucent and looked like a jewel. The red ones looked like rubies. The blue ones looked like sapphires. They were gorgeous. As for the ceramic beads, each bead was a work of art. There were mermaid-shaped beads, leaf-shaped beads, sun and moon-shaped beads... These glass and ceramic beads, which were normally very expensive, were now virtually free. I thought about buying forty glass beads to make a Bardonian mala. Imagine a Bardonian mala that looked like a string of jewels! Normally, these beads would have been too expensive for me to buy, but now I could get them by paying a trivial amount of money. I thought about buying twenty red glass beads and twenty blue glass beads so I could make an electric and magnetic fluid-themed Bardonian mala by alternating the bead colors. I also thought about combining a mermaid-shaped ceramic bead with alternating light blue and dark blue glass beads to create a water element-themed Bardonain mala. I even thought about buying forty beads of various colors to make a rainbow TMO-themed Bardonian mala.

Then, I realized something. Although the Bardonian mala I was currently using was made of cheap plastic beads, it served its purpose well. And, if my current Bardonian mala serves its purpose well, why do I need to make another one?

Any time I'd spend making a Bardonian mala out of those glass and ceramic beads would be better spent practicing Type 1 or Type 2 exercises. I walked out of the store without buying any of the glass and ceramic beads, even though they were virtually free.

Chapter 49

A Less Well-Known Fact

I t is a well-known fact that practicing the mental exercises in Mouni Sadhu's book *Concentration: A Guide to Mental Mastery* will help you master the mental exercises in IIH. It is a less well-known fact that practicing the mental exercises in IIH will also help you master the mental exercises in IIH.

Chapter 50

Don't Lie to Yourself

W hen it comes to magical training, perhaps the single worst thing you can do to yourself is lie to yourself. In one of the most popular posts on my blog, I discuss the difference between making a half-hearted attempt at practicing an exercise and using your whole heart. One example I give in that post is introspection, explaining why many of the students who think they are introspecting wholeheartedly are actually doing a half-hearted job, unbeknownst to themselves. If you are practicing an exercise half-heartedly, don't lie to yourself by telling yourself that you are practicing the exercise wholeheartedly. I'm sure you can imagine how lying to yourself in this manner will ensure you will never master the exercise. Bardonists lie to themselves all the time. This is one common reason many of them are bound to remain stuck on Step 1 for many years. Here are some examples of Bardonists who are lying to themselves.

Tom has found a chakra exercise in a New Age book. He wants to practice the exercise because it seems interesting; however, he knows that this is not a good reason to spend his limited time practicing an exercise. Because of this, he tells himself that the exercise would be a good supplement to his Bardon system training and then goes on to practice the exercise. Tom is lying to himself.

Suzie has found a book about the work of KTQ. She wants to read the book because it seems interesting; however, she knows that she should read the books she needs to read rather than the books she merely wants to read. As a result, she tells herself that she needs to read this book because she is a

Bardonist and the book is related to the Bardon system. She then goes on to read the book. Suzie is lying to herself.

Greg is interested in the Golden Dawn system. He really wants to work through the Golden Dawn system in addition to working through IIH; however, he knows that successfully working through a magical training system requires that you be focused, and that you cannot be focused on two things at the same time. Greg tells himself that if he were to train in the Golden Dawn system, this training would supplement the training he was already doing in the Bardon system, thus helping him advance through IIH faster. As a result, Greg begins working through the Golden Dawn system. Greg is lying to himself.

Many times, a Bardonist corresponding with me will tell me about all the outside exercises he is practicing in addition to the exercises within IIH. I will then ask "Do you really need to be doing those exercises?" Often, they will reply in the affirmative. This is how I know they are lying to themselves.

Don't get me wrong. I am not against practicing outside exercises. I am only against practicing outside exercises that are Type 3, Type 4, or Type 5 exercises. When I see that the outside exercises a Bardonist is practicing are Type 2 exercises, I don't ask that question, but encourage them to continue supplementing their Bardon system training with those outside exercises. However, in the vast majority of cases, the outside exercises a Bardonist is practicing are not Type 2 exercises. When Bardonists tell me that the Type 3, Type 4, and Type 5 exercises they are doing are exercises they need to be doing, I know it is not me they are lying to, but themselves.

Chapter 51

The Pareto Principle

I f you're like most Bardonists, the Pareto principle applies to many aspects of your magical training.

Eighty percent of the books you read aren't really doing anything for you. Only twenty percent of the books you read are actually helping you. That twenty percent consists of the books that are actually relevant to your training. If you're on Step 1, any books you read about mindfulness, introspection, or getting your life organized would fall into the twenty percent. Any books you read about Qabalah, the Enochian calls, or ritual magic would fall into the eighty percent.

Eighty percent of the exercises you practice aren't really doing anything for you. Only twenty percent of the exercises you practice are actually helping you. That twenty percent consists of the Type 1 and Type 2 exercises. All other exercises fall into the eighty percent.

Chapter 52

Tidying Up

There's a good chance you've heard of Marie Kondo's book *The Life-Changing Magic of Tidying Up*. In fact, you might even be familiar with the revolutionary approach to organizing that the book teaches. According to Kondo, before you try to organize your house, you must first throw out everything that isn't worth keeping. Otherwise, you'll end up organizing things that shouldn't even be in your house.

To make efficient progress along the magical path, your training must be organized. To organize your training, you must first throw out everything that isn't worth keeping. Throw out all of the Type 3/4/5 exercises like the Qabalistic pathworkings, New Age chakra exercises, and Golden Dawn rituals (e.g. the LBRP). You might think they do a good job of supplementing your Bardon system training, but they don't. Throw out all of the books not relevant to your training, like the books on ritual magic, the books on Thelema, and the books on Solomonic evocation. Marie Kondo says if it doesn't spark joy, throw it out. I say if it doesn't really help you in your training, throw it out.

Chapter 53

Your Advancement is in Your Hands

When corresponding with Bardonists who reach out to me, I often say things like the following.

Every minute you spend practicing the LBRP is a minute you could be spending practicing thought-observation.

Every minute you spend studying Qabalah is a minute you could be spending studying yourself (AKA introspecting).

Every minute you spend angrily arguing on a Bardon forum is a minute you could be spending using conscious breathing to develop patience.

Every minute you spend practicing some chakra exercise you found in a New Age book is a minute you could be spending practicing the exercises of IIH.

Every minute you spend reading an article about meditation is a minute you could be spending actually meditating.

For some people, the LBRP is more fun than thought-observation, studying Qabalah is more interesting than studying yourself, and practicing a New Age chakra exercise is easier than practicing the intense elemental energy-work exercises of IIH. However, if you want to reach adepthood, then you have to do what you need to do in order to reach adepthood. It doesn't matter if what you need to do is not fun, or not interesting, or not easy. If you have to do it, then you have to do it.

If you spend time doing the LBRP, or studying Qabalah, or arguing on the internet, or practicing some chakra exercise, or reading an article about meditation, it's not because someone else made you do it. It's because you chose to do it. How quickly you advance depends on what choices you make regarding how to use your time. You make your choices, so your advancement is in your own hands and no one else's.

Chapter 54

Keep Your Approach Simple and Focused

Anytime you want to reach a big goal like adepthood, you need to have a system that will get you there. As Bardonists, we do have a system – the Bardon system. However, although a system is necessary, it's not enough. All Bardonists have the Bardon system, but not all Bardonists will reach adepthood. Any system can be approached in different ways. To reach adepthood, you not only need the Bardon system, you also need an effective approach. For me, an effective approach is a simple and focused approach.

- Practice the exercises of IIH every day.
- If you have extra time, practice Type 2 exercises.
- When you decide to do a bit of reading, only read books that are relevant to you at your current stage of training.
- Avoid wasting your time and energy.
- Write the number 1440 on a piece of paper and tape it over your desk. Look at it whenever you're tempted to go on social media, watch television, or read comics.
- Poop mindfully and protect your time by being assertive.
- Don't lie to yourself, strengthen your vasanas, or act greedy.
- Travel light, discriminate, and have respect for yourself.

- Tidy up every now and then; start by letting go of what you don't need.
- Make wise choices and see things exactly as they are.

And there you have it. That's a simple and focused approach. Use it, and it will take you far.

Chapter 55

For Those Who Spend Their Whole Lives Stuck on Step 1

Some people will move through Step 1 in a timely manner. Other people will spend many years stuck on Step 1. A handful of people will even spend their whole lives stuck on Step 1. If you find at the end of your incarnation that you have spent your whole life stuck on Step 1, you may feel that you have wasted your time. This isn't necessarily true. Reflect back on your life and identify the specific mistakes you made that prevented you from moving on to Step 2 and kept you stuck on Step 1 your entire life. Then, write a book describing those mistakes in great detail. Send the manuscript of the book to Falcon Books Publishing and we will publish it. Do not worry if English is not your native language. The Falcon Books Publishing team has some great editors who can proofread your manuscript, help with revisions, and make sure it is polished and free of errors.

Your book will be a valuable resource for future Bardonists. By identifying the mistakes that kept you stuck on Step 1 your whole life and describing them in your book, those who read your book will learn about those mistakes and know to avoid them in their own training. You might have spent your whole life stuck on Step 1, but by sharing the knowledge you gained from the mistakes you made, you can help ensure that others won't make those same mistakes and also spend their whole lives stuck on Step 1. Writing such a book is a wonderful act of service, and many generations of future Bardonists will be grateful to you for your efforts.

Appendix 1: A Note Regarding Brahmacharya

I mention in the first chapter that brahmacharya is often defined as celibacy. This definition is ok for yogis, but not for magicians. Brahmacharya is really about not wasting your energy. For a yogi, energy spent having sex may be wasted, but this is not the case for the aspiring magician. The reason is explained well in the following passage from one of Bill Mistele's essays.

> But if this distinction between higher and lower somehow implies that material desires are somehow of lesser importance in life, some of the lunar spirits would immediately stand up and object. From their point of view, the material universe has been created in order to celebrate love. You are going against the laws of the universe and generating karma if you leave physical happiness and gratification out of your equation for the meaning and purpose of life. If you seek the physical and ignore the spirit, you generate horrible karma. If you seek the spirit and ignore the physical, you generate horrible karma. This is because the two are a part of the same design.
>
> For example, in the scheme of things, enjoying sex is just as important as communing with God. If you do the "higher" at the expense of the "lower" you have a demon waiting for you behind a door and he is slowing prying out the hinges and

picking the lock in order to get to you. This is because God created that demon to remind you of the importance of sexuality as a key to discovering who you are. The demon's authority and commission are activated by your act of repression. The demon represents your blind spot--an essential area of life which you have written off as unworthy of your attention.

If you pursue sex at the expense of communing with God, there is another demon waiting for you. His power derives from the creativity in life you have left behind because if anything God is creative and that power is the essence of your being. This demon haunts an abyss of haos. He is authorized to bring that chaos into your life. The reason is that divine creativity is unafraid of emptiness and any abyss. It seeks them out because that is the space of the imagination which it requires to create. The creator is unafraid and freely and willingly enters the unknown in order to make something new.

While yoga is a path of ascetism, magic is a path of balance. It advocates moderation in sex, and not complete abstinence. Energy spent having sex is not wasted because, among other reasons, it prevents you from suffering the negative effects of sexual repression. However, having sex more often than you need to is a waste of energy. Of course, it's ok (but not necessary) to waste energy every now and then, as long as you monitor your energy level and make sure you still have enough for your training. Oscar Wilde once said "Everything in moderation, including moderation." Some people might find that this quote resonates with them.

Appendix 2: An Interpretation of "Simple Gifts"

This book's title is inspired by the song "Simple Gifts." I'd like to share some of the things that come to mind when I reflect on the lyrics of this song. Bear with me here. I'm not trying to imply that Joseph Brackett was an esotericist or that he was knowledgeable about runes. I just want to show how finding an interpretation of the song relevant to my own path has helped me.

'Tis the gift to be simple, 'tis the gift to be free

It truly is a gift to have a simple approach to working through IIH, because a simple approach is an effective one. People often brag about how complicated their training is. They brag about how they have combined the Bardon system and the Golden Dawn system and are practicing this mess as if it were somehow superior to practicing the Bardon system alone in its simplicity. They brag about how they have added a bunch of exercises from Dzogchen and Huna into their daily practice routine, in addition to the exercises of IIH. They brag about how they are studying a dozen or so books each week about metaphysics and spirituality. The people who brag about these things don't have the gift - the gift to be simple.

It is also a gift to be free - free from all the clutter that weighs one down, and that was described in Chapter 43.

Tis the gift to come down where we ought to be,

It's a gift to come down from the high realms of fantasy and delusion. People think that by adding a bunch of unnecessary exercises to their daily practice routine, or by studying many books about the Bardon system, they will advance quickly. This is a fantasy, and people need to come down from that fantasy and into the world of reality, where it is clear that a simple approach is a focused approach and a focused approach is an effective approach.

And when we find ourselves in the place just right, '

Twill be in the valley of love and delight.

After you have freed yourself from the fantasy that the cluttered and complicated is superior to the simple and focused, you can settle down into a simple approach that works for you. Training tends to be unnecessarily stressful if your approach is unnecessarily complicated. A simple approach leads to enjoyment of your training and delight in the actual progress you are making.

When true simplicity is gained,

To bow and to bend we shan't be ashamed,

When we find a simple and focused approach, we will not be ashamed to "bow." That is to say, we will not be ashamed to be humble, because we realize that arrogance is detrimental to magical advancement. Again, a simple approach is a focused approach. When we are focused on our training, we realize that it is more important to train than to waste time and energy building up a facade of being a great adept or advanced Bardonist.

We will also not be ashamed to "bend." That is to say, we will be willing to avoid arrogant people and get out of their way. Rather than compete with them when they brag about how advanced they are or how complicated their approaches to training are, we will instead ignore them and direct all of our attention to our own training.

To turn, turn will be our delight,

The rune associated with turning is Jera. Since Jera is associated with turning, it is also associated with cycles. Each turn of Jera represents the completion of one cycle. Usually, this cycle refers to the turning of the Earth. Thus, each turn of Jera refers to one rotation of the Earth. In the context of magical training, each turn of Jera refers to the completion of one round of one's daily practice routine. Wake up and repeat an autosuggestion affirmation forty times. Meditate for twenty minutes. Practice conscious eating at breakfast and lunch. Practice conscious breathing in the afternoon after getting home from work and then pray a little. Practice conscious eating at dinner, and then magical washing while showering. Meditate again for twenty minutes before going to bed. Repeat the autosuggestion affirmation forty times again as you're falling asleep. This is an example of a possible daily practice routine for someone on Step 1.

Turning once will not get you to adepthood. You must turn every day, but don't worry. Turning will be your delight. In other words, if you train right, then training should be fun.

Till by turning, turning we come 'round right.

Magical training is a process of becoming pure and balanced. It is a process of becoming "right." Every time you turn, you become a little more right. If you turn enough, you will be fully right.

Bibliography

Atteshlis, Stylianos. *The Esoteric Practice: Christian Meditations and Exercises*. Imprinta, 1994.

Brahm, Ajahn. *The Art of Disappearing: Buddhas Path to Lasting Joy*. Wisdom Publications, 2011.

Godman, David. "Remembering Nisargadatta Maharaj - Page 4 of 10." David Godman, July 12, 2019. https://www.davidgodman.org/remembering-nisargadatta-maharaj/4/.

Han , Thich Nhat. "The Fifth Precept: Diet for a Mindful Society." *Bhikshuni Thubten Chodron*, thubtenchodron.org/2017/11/non-harmful-consumption-not-intoxicants/.

Kruse, Kevin. *15 Secrets Successful People Know about Time Management: the Productivity Habits of 7 Billionaires, 13 Olympic Athletes, 29 Straight-A Students, and 239 Entrepreneurs*. The Kruse Group, 2017.

Markides, Kyriacos C. *The Magus of Strovolos: the Extraordinary World of a Spiritual Healer*. Arkana, 1998.

Mistele, William. "Franz Bardon Hermetics, Fairy Tales, and Transpersonal Psychology." *Bardon Home Page*, www.williammistele.com/.

Priddy, Brad. "Yama and Niyama." *Yama and Niyama*, www.bradpriddy.com/yoga/yamani.htm.